Nativism, Nationalism, and Patriotism

Other Books in the Current Controversies Series

Nativism, Nationalism, and Patriotism

Eamon Doyle, Book Editor

GREENHAVEN
PUBLISHING

Published in 2021 by Greenhaven Publishing, LLC
353 3rd Avenue, Suite 255, New York, NY 10010

First Edition

Articles in Greenhaven Publishing anthologies are often edited for length to meet page
requirements. In addition, original titles of these works are changed to clearly present
the main thesis and to explicitly indicate the author's opinion. Every effort is made to
ensure that Greenhaven Publishing accurately reflects the original intent of the authors.
Every effort has been made to trace the owners of the copyrighted material.

Cover image: Motortion Films/Shutterstock.com

Library of Congress Cataloging-in-Publication Data

Names: Doyle, Eamon, editor.
Title: Nativism, nationalism, and patriotism / Eamon Doyle, book editor.
Description: First edition. | New York : Greenhaven Publishing, 2021. | Series: Current
  controversies | Includes bibliographic references and index. | Audience: Grades 9–12.
Identifiers: ISBN 9781534507005 (library binding) | ISBN 9781534506992 (paperback)
Subjects: LCSH: Nationalism—Juvenile literature. | Patriotism—Juvenile literature.
| Nationalism—United States—Juvenile literature. | Patriotism—United States—
Juvenile literature. | National characteristics—Juvenile literature. | Nativism.
Classification: LCC JC311.N388 2021 | DDC 320.540973—dc23

Manufactured in the United States of America

Website: http://greenhavenpublishing.com

Contents

Chapter 1: Are Nationalist Ideals Compatible with Liberal Democracy?

Tedd Siegel

In this excerpted viewpoint, Siegel looks at the moral and epistemic dimensions of modern life to illustrate why there is sometimes tension between nationalist and liberal democratic ideas.

Yes: There Is No Essential Conflict Between Liberal Democracy and Nationalism

Marc Saxer

Saxer examines the recent association between patriotism and the politics of the right and looks at historical examples that show how patriotism can function as a medium of expression for liberal and left-wing ideologies as well.

E. J. Dionne

E. J. Dionne analyzes a 2019 book on nationalism in the United States by influential political journalist John Judis. He spotlights Judis's argument that American progressives have been stubbornly resistant to incorporating—and leveraging—nationalistic attitudes into their rhetorical culture, which has limited their effectiveness politically.

Marc Plattner

Plattner rejects the idea that nationalism is essentially antidemocratic. He points to historical examples that show how nationalism, properly understood, can actually work to support democratic political attitudes and behavior.

In this excerpted viewpoint, Wilkin looks at the global history of nationalist movements and explores how diverse forms of nationalist sentiment—including nativist/xenophobic strains as well as more benign patriotic examples—emerged during the twentieth century.

Yes: Nationalism, Nativism, and Patriotism Are Not the Same

No: Nativism, Nationalism, and Patriotism Are Closely Related and Often Interchangeable Concepts

Cobb and McCoy throw a spotlight on the historical similarities between nationalism and nativism, particularly in terms of their association with xenophobia and ethnic or racial discrimination. The authors argue that efforts to distinguish them distract from their shared bigotry and discriminatory manifestations.

Chapter 3: Does the Global Rise of Nationalism Mean the End of Liberal Democracy?

Yes: The Rise of Nationalism Indicates the Decline of Liberal Democracy

Sandra Waddock

For much of the twentieth century and into the beginning of the twenty-first, neoliberalism typified most Western democracies. Neoliberalism is largely characterized by free market capitalism and a hands-off approach to economics, but income inequality and market collapses have shifted voters toward populist and nationalist candidates. Liberal democratic movements that support universal well-being can counter the move toward illiberal populism.

Foreword

"Controversy" is a word that has an undeniably unpleasant connotation. It carries a definite negative charge. Controversy can spoil family gatherings, spread a chill around classroom and campus discussion, inflame public discourse, open raw civic wounds, and lead to the ouster of public officials. We often feel that controversy is almost akin to bad manners, a rude and shocking eruption of that which must not be spoken or thought of in polite, tightly guarded society. To avoid controversy, to quell controversy, is often seen as a public good, a victory for etiquette, perhaps even a moral or ethical imperative.

Yet the studious, deliberate avoidance of controversy is also a whitewashing, a denial, a death threat to democracy. It is a false sterilizing and sanitizing and superficial ordering of the messy, ragged, chaotic, at times ugly processes by which a healthy democracy identifies and confronts challenges, engages in passionate debate about appropriate approaches and solutions, and arrives at something like a consensus and a broadly accepted and supported way forward. Controversy is the megaphone, the speaker's corner, the public square through which the citizenry finds and uses its voice. Controversy is the life's blood of our democracy and absolutely essential to the vibrant health of our society.

Our present age is certainly no stranger to controversy. We are consumed by fierce debates about technology, privacy, political correctness, poverty, violence, crime and policing, guns, immigration, civil and human rights, terrorism, militarism, environmental protection, and gender and racial equality. Loudly competing voices are raised every day, shouting opposing opinions, putting forth competing agendas, and summoning starkly different visions of a utopian or dystopian future. Often these voices attempt to shout the others down; there is precious little listening and considering among the cacophonous din. Yet listening and considering, too, are essential to the health of a democracy. If controversy is democracy's lusty lifeblood, respectful listening and careful thought are its higher faculties, its brain, its conscience.

Current Controversies does not shy away from or attempt to hush the loudly competing voices. It seeks to provide readers with as wide and representative as possible a range of articulate voices on any given controversy of the day, separates each one out to allow it to be heard clearly and fairly, and encourages careful listening to each of these well-crafted, thoughtfully expressed opinions, supplied by some of today's leading academics, thinkers, analysts, politicians, policy makers, economists, activists, change agents, and advocates. Only after listening to a wide range of opinions on an issue, evaluating the strengths and weaknesses of each argument, assessing how well the facts and available evidence mesh with the stated opinions and conclusions, and thoughtfully and critically examining one's own beliefs and conscience can the reader begin to arrive at his or her own conclusions and articulate his or her own stance on the spotlighted controversy.

This process is facilitated and supported in each Current Controversies volume by an introduction and chapter overviews that provide readers with the essential context they need to begin engaging with the spotlighted controversies, with the debates surrounding them, and with their own perhaps shifting or nascent opinions on them. Chapters are organized around several key questions that are answered with diverse opinions representing all points on the political spectrum. In its content, organization, and methodology, readers are encouraged to determine the authors' point of view and purpose, interrogate and analyze the various arguments and their rhetoric and structure, evaluate the arguments' strengths and weaknesses, test their claims against available facts and evidence, judge the validity of the reasoning, and bring into clearer, sharper focus the reader's own beliefs and conclusions and how they may differ from or align with those in the collection or those of classmates.

Research has shown that reading comprehension skills improve dramatically when students are provided with compelling, intriguing, and relevant "discussable" texts. The subject matter of these collections could not be more compelling, intriguing, or urgently relevant to today's students and the world they are poised to inherit. The anthologized articles also provide the basis for stimulating, lively, and passionate classroom debates. Students who are compelled to anticipate objections to their own argument and identify the flaws in those of an opponent read more carefully, think more critically, and steep themselves in relevant context, facts, and information more thoroughly. In short, using discussable text of the kind provided by every single volume in the Current Controversies series encourages close reading, facilitates reading comprehension, fosters research, strengthens critical thinking, and greatly enlivens and energizes classroom discussion and participation. The entire learning process is deepened, extended, and strengthened.

If we are to foster a knowledgeable, responsible, active, and engaged citizenry, we must provide readers with the intellectual, interpretive, and critical-thinking tools and experience necessary to make sense of the world around them and of the all-important debates and arguments that inform it. We must encourage them not to run away from or attempt to quell controversy but to embrace it in a responsible, conscientious, and thoughtful way, to sharpen and strengthen their own informed opinions by listening to and critically analyzing those of others. This series encourages respectful engagement with and analysis of current controversies and competing opinions and fosters a resulting increase in the strength and rigor of one's own opinions and stances. As such, it helps readers assume their rightful place in the public square and provides them with the skills necessary to uphold their awesome responsibility—guaranteeing the continued and future health of a vital, vibrant, and free democracy.

Introduction

> *"During the twentieth century, men fought on behalf of nationalism. Yet the wars they fought were also engendered by dislocations in world markets and by social revolution stimulated by the coming of the industrial age."*
>
> *-Zbigniew Brzezinski, Polish-American diplomat and political scientist*

At the end of the twentieth century, many experts were convinced that the momentum behind the global expansion of liberal democracy had become inexorable. There was simply too much energy behind the core ideas of individual freedom and open markets to imagine a recession of their influence. The political scientist Francis Fukuyama crystalized this perspective in his well-known 1992 study *The End of History and the Last Man*:

> What we may be witnessing is not just the end of the Cold War, or the passing of a particular period of post-war history, but the end of history as such[...]that is, the end point of mankind's ideological evolution and the universalization of Western liberal democracy as the final form of human government.[1]

But the events of the past several years—such as the 2016 Brexit referendum, the 2016 election of President Trump in the United States, and a global wave of authoritarian populist politics in Russia, Hungary, Turkey, the Philippines, and elsewhere—have thrown Fukuyama's theory into doubt and led to renewed interest in the political alternatives to liberal democracy, especially nationalism.

Nationalism had been largely out of fashion in mainstream Western politics since World War II, which it was widely viewed as having played a role in causing. In general, its reputation was strongly associated with dubious racial and ethnic theories, authoritarian political leaders, and imperial expansionism. John Hutchinson, a professor of government at the London School of Economics, writes:

> Critics say that nationalism is historical fantasy: such nations have not existed before the modern world, human populations more often than not have been intermingled, and attempts to separate them into exclusive territories generates conflict. [Nationalist] leaders create external enemies, thereby diverting the violence inherent in human beings outwards rather than towards the powers that be. [2]

Nationalism—like liberalism and socialism—is a fundamentally modern ideology and a direct outgrowth of the development of the modern nation-state in the post-Enlightenment era. It distinguishes itself from liberalism by elevating values like solidarity, social cohesion, and national strength over values based on individual rights, particularly freedom of speech, protest, and religion. And it distinguishes itself from globalism, cosmopolitanism, and internationalism in its suspicion toward diplomatic cooperation and its conception of nations as fundamentally competitive—as opposed to potentially cooperative—entities.

However, there is a psychological component to nationalism as well, one that involves group identification and attachment to a specific place or homeland. Hutchinson, for instance, defines nationalism partly as a type of secular religion:

> Nationalism is a secular 'religion' that proclaims that the world is composed of unique and ancient nations which have exclusive homelands, and that the sacred duty of individuals is to defend the territory, independence, and identity of their nation. [3]

Proponents celebrate the quasi-religious, fantasy-driven aspects of nationalism in terms of the identification they facilitate between the individual and the state, and the connection between such identification and the broader solidarity of the nation. The concept of patriotism is often invoked to describe positive aspects of this participatory dimension of nationalist politics. The influential writer John Fonte exemplifies this close association between nationalism and patriotism:

> If patriotism is completely divorced from nationalism, then patriotism itself will be hollowed out, an empty shell. This is the inevitable result of the "patriotism good, nationalism bad" argument. Anti-nationalism leads to anti-patriotism except for the most cold, abstract variety of what remains of "patriotism." [...] At the end of the day, to paraphrase Ben Franklin, patriotism and nationalism will either hang together, or they will hang separately, both diluted and diminished. [4]

But nationalism and patriotism have more than their share of critics, including some who describe both as a vehicle for various forms of nativism, racism, and xenophobia.

In some ways, this perception has to do with the fundamental distinction at the heart of nationalism—between members of the nation community and non-members. When ideological influences dispose human beings to separate other humans into groups on an "us vs. them" basis, the risk of such distinctions being drawn along racial or ethnic lines is very significant. The journalist Mona Charen writes:

> Nationalism is a demagogue's patriotism. [Nationalists] argue that our troubles are the result of immigrants' taking our jobs or foreigners' stealing our factories. This is not natural love of home and hearth or reverence for America's founding ideals; it is scapegoating. [5]

Charen and others have plenty of evidence on their side. Many prominent examples of nationalist politics in action come from autocratic or totalitarian regimes that enforced policies of exclusion, discrimination, and even genocide. Whether demagoguery and scapegoating constitute essential features of nationalism is an open question. But what is abundantly clear is that the world is witnessing an unexpected resurgence of ideas that appeared defunct no more than a few years ago. Although the extent and impact of this resurgence remain to be seen, Prasenjit Duara, a professor of East Asian history at Duke University, takes a distinctly pessimistic view:

> Nationalism in Europe and Asia has had many faces: revolutionary, top-down, anti-communist, participatory, civic, ethnic, and religious. The immediate post-war decades saw a largely inclusive civic model across much of the globe, permitting new nation-states to develop capabilities and resources without strong ethnocentric biases. More recently, the relationship between national political movements and economic development has taken a more sinister turn. [...] The global ascendance of neoliberal capitalism has been accompanied by the rise of chauvinistic, populist nationalism. The connection between nationalism and development appears to have come full cycle from a century ago, when its darkest forms drove the world into two global conflicts. [6]

The coming decades of human history will determine whether Duara's pessimism is warranted. In the meantime, *Current Controversies: Nativism, Nationalism, and Patriotism* aims to make sense of these concepts and the role they play in global politics through the lens of a wide variety of viewpoints.

Notes

1. Francis Fukuyama. *The End of History and the Last Man*. New York: Avon Books, 1992.

2. John Hutchinson. *Does Nationalism Cause War?* Oxford University Press, February 4, 2018.

3. John Hutchinson. *Does Nationalism Cause War?* Oxford University Press, February 4, 2018.

4. John Fonte. "American Patriotism and Nationalism: One and Indivisible." *National Review*, May 1, 2017.

5. Mona Charen. "Patriotism Not Nationalism." *National Review*, February 17, 2017.

6. Prasenjit Duara. "Development and the Crisis of Global Nationalism." The Brookings Institution, October 4, 2018.

CHAPTER 1

Are Nationalist Ideals Compatible with Liberal Democracy?

The Prospect of Civic Nationalism

Tedd Siegel

Tedd Siegel is a writer and philosopher who works in strategic partnership management, primarily in the semiconductor industry in Silicon Valley. He is interested in the moral and epistemic foundations of modern life.

[...]

In his excellent article from 2016, "America Is Not a Nation," In Dark Times' own Steve Heikkila forcefully challenged the claim of the new American white ethno-nationalist nativism that it somehow intersects with the tradition of American patriotism.

In his article, Heikkila reminds us of Hannah Arendt's 1973 interview where she says that the USA is united "neither by heritage, nor by memory, nor by soil, nor by language," but rather by common citizenship, and this "through their consent to the constitution." Americans are Americans, she argues, "because they have chosen to be so."

To seek to transform the children of immigrants into American nativists, Heikkila continues, runs counter to the spirit of 1776, and is thus an attempt to fabricate something that simply doesn't exist. Instead, he argues, the "patrie" of American patriotism was founded by an act of political choice, so that the shared identity of Americans is premised upon a shared oath (actual on the part of immigrants, implied for those born here) to honor a set of political ideals deriving from the American creed of liberal democracy.

In this article, I am seeking to explore what can be seen to lie behind this constitutional patriotism with its foundation in political voluntarism, and what also can be seen to flow from it—namely a "desire to live together" as Ernest Renan famously wrote, but in a (politically and socially) particular way. Steve Heikkila dares us to

"Civic Nationalism & Democratic Social Solidarity," by Tedd Siegel, In Dark Times, January 19, 2019. https://www.indarktimes.com/civic-nationalism-democratic-social-solidarity. Used by permission.

remember that because America is founded in freedom, Americans are not Americans because of historically determined factors out of their control. Americans as such are "a collection of individuals united by little more than their mutual consent to a social contract."

What does it mean to ground a national identity in a shared voluntary political commitment to live according to a certain set of principles? In recent years, this sort of constitutional patriotism has been largely scoffed at as being simply too thin to bear the weight of something like a national identity. My jumping off point, however, is where Heikkila writes that this sort of patriotism is "closer to Rousseau's civil religion in *The Social Contract.*"

By looking at Theda Skocpol's *Diminished Democracy,* I am interested to explore the experience of civic nationalism that gives both dimension and an element of solidarity to this constitutional patriotic form of allegiance. It is my conviction that while it's true to say that Americans are united by "little more than their mutual consent" this *little more* points to a backdrop of a distinctive history and experience of civic nationalism that anchors our political voluntarism in social solidarity. It is my view that when seen in this way, the *little more* turns out to be *just enough.*

It is important to note that the last time the question of civic nationalism was debated with great urgency in the early 1990s, international legal and political theorists were especially worried about managing the expectations of nationalist succession movements by various ethnic minorities after the breakup of the Soviet Union (along with other long-festering claims to national self-determination by minority citizens in mature states).

As Michael Walzer explained in his introduction to *Thick and Thin: Moral Argument & Home and Abroad* (1994), the name of the game was to try to find some resolution to the problem posed by the idea of the nation-state itself, to find a balanced way to insist on and otherwise promote democratic principles of government while also being committed to cultural autonomy and national independence, or to quote him directly, "…to endorse a certain politics of difference while defending a certain sort of universalism."

Beneath the laudable aspiration announced here, namely to be both enlightened and caring, (and thus to "have the cake, but to eat it too") there was always some sense that ethnic nationalism existed, like a brain fever, mostly in places where a democratic, civic nationalism had not yet firmly established itself (as long as one forgot about places like Northern Ireland, Quebec, and India, of course). Put another way, the search for some sort of middle passage (if not for an outright "cure") for ethnic nationalism generally rested, as Bernard Yack has written, on the assumption that "in western democracies, freely chosen principles have replaced cultural heritage as the basis of cultural solidarity."

Writing a year earlier than Walzer, in *Blood and Belonging*, Michael Ignatieff, for example, remarks that "while the psychology of [ethnic] belonging may have greater depth than civic nationalism's…the sociology that accompanies it is a good deal less realistic." Ignatieff here concurs with others proponents of civic nationalism from this period who (again, per Bernard Yack) would debunk "the national myths that exaggerate the virtues of nations and otherwise distort the historical record, inflaming passions that ignite ethnic conflicts…and remind us that nations are imagined communities or constructed or invented rather than simply handed down."

In the later 90s and early 2000s, however, civic nationalism and its proponents, including those making the case for a so-called "constitutional patriotism" took quite a beating. For example, in her 1999 paper "The False Promise of Civic Nationalism" Chimène Keitner argued that civic nationalism, as a purported form of nationalism, must be evaluated (along with ethnic nationalism) by the extent to which it "provides something more than just a state-based account of identity and allegiance." With this in mind, Keitner interrogates civic nationalism in order to find the "account of pre-political identity that it offers for establishing the viability of political arrangements," but all she is able to find are accounts of state patriotism that try unsuccessfully, she writes, to "harness the pre-political bonds of solidarity characteristic of nations while associating them with the institutions of the state."

In urging identification with republican, state-based values, Keitner says, civic nationalists effectively collapse the distinction between nation and state, and the arguments that deliberative democracy theorists like Habermas make for their constitutional patriotism (based on formal procedural agreement and principles of mutual respect) amount to a cosmopolitanism that is "not robust enough to nourish and sustain states as distinct political and territorial entities."

In "The Myth of Civic Nationalism" (2000) Bernard Yack argued something similar, writing that "civic nationalism is really just wishful thinking" because it "turns national belonging into a form of rational attachment, a choice rather than a legacy." Even if it's true that national communities are largely imagined, Yack says, "they are imagined by groups trying to work things out in the present, not by individuals making voluntarist rationalist commitments."

It is my view that these critics, concerned with the pesky problem of the nation-state for emerging democracies in far flung corners of the world, and serenely confident that nationalism represented no significant threat to mature democracies, have actually missed something quite important by not trying harder to characterize the "pre-political aspect" of post-nationalist constitutionally patriotic solidarity. The current unprecedented rise of neo-nationalism in mature, Western democracies like the USA places the question of civil society once again at the heart of both theoretical and practical concern–but this time with an unexpected twist. The twist is that this time, a compelling account of our own tradition of civic nationalism is urgently needed in order to combat the rise of a mythic white ethno-nationalism.

Why should it be so difficult to describe the solidarity of constitutionally patriotic citizens for whom the nation is a shared democratic civic life? The "post-nationalist nation" is a community with shared thin notions of the good. While it is certainly possible to theorize these ethical and political commitments in ideal terms, I have a sense that it is also possible to locate this commitment in the real experience of American civic life.

[...]

Reclaiming Patriotism for Liberals and Social Democrats

Marc Saxer

Marc Saxer is a German political analyst and resident representative of the Friedrich-Ebert-Stiftung (FES) in their India office. Previously, he served at FES in the "Dialogues on Globalization" program.

The fear of social decline takes hold in all parts of society. Feeling at the mercy of the anonymous forces of globalisation, automation and migration, many are turning inwards in order to at least get their own lives under control. Yet this retreat makes communal spaces shrink further, where people once felt they were shaping their own surroundings together. The dwindling trust in the power of politics to shape society has also been eroded by the withdrawal of the state. Many people feel left in the lurch, and are looking to political alternatives beyond the democratic centre.

Enter right-wing populism: The new right offers protection and stability to all those who feel unheard by lobby-dominated post-democracies, left behind by the rapid economic changes and ignored by pluralistic society in general and the liberal elites in particular.

To beat right-wing populism, politicians need to put more effort into restoring people's control over their lives and their sense of community and belonging to society. This takes more than material security. People need an identity that gives them the pride, recognition and self-esteem to be able to engage with a fast-changing world. Therefore, social democracy has to offer an identity to all those who are looking for protection and belonging.

So far, social democracy has failed to counter the nativist rhetoric of right-wing populists with a progressive concept of

"Progressive patriotism: Progressives have ceded patriotism to the right. It's high time they reclaim it to end austerity and restore public services," by Marc Saxer, International Politics and Society, February 5, 2019. Reprinted by permission.

identity. On one hand, progressives fear opening a Pandora's box of nationalism, opening the gates to racism and xenophobia. On the other hand, they argue that too much identity politics and too little attention to redistribution has alienated the white working class.

The Dilemma of Progressivism

Both arguments fall short. First, social democracy never shied away from drawing on the emotional energy of collective identities. In the days of the labour movement, institutions from hiking clubs and choirs to gymnastics groups were essential in building the awareness of the working class. Second, we can see from the central political conflicts of the 21st century—from immigration ("rapefugees") to gender equality ("#metoo")—that conflicts of material distribution are fought out under the guise of culture. If progressives are unable to express their position in a language that resonates with these new debates, then their arguments will go unheard. And ultimately, the progressives' surrender of collective identity politics has left the field wide open for right-wing populists.

Tactical arguments are by no means the only ones in favour of a progressive concept of identity. The heart of social democracy, the community of solidarity, is ineffective without a framework of identity. If it's unclear who belongs to the community and who doesn't, it also remains unclear who should share something with whom. That's a central dilemma of all progressive projects: redistribution is more effective between members of smaller, mutually supportive communities. Today however, the distributive struggles over resources need to be won against capital which acts on a global scale.

This dilemma shows the different directions in which progressives want to take their projects. Left-wing nationalists are pushing for a return to the nation-state. Strategically, the common frame of the nation is supposed unite isolated struggles of particular interest groups. Before the nation can be put to such use, however, left nationalists must first wrest ownership of this problematic term from the right. To achieve this, they propose a different form of demarcation. Where the nationalist right-wingers set "the people" apart from "outsiders," progressives conceive "the people" (99 per cent) as the opposite of the "elite" (1 per cent). This way, they hope to save the democratic national welfare state from being totally worn down by global capital and technocrats in Brussels.

By contrast, internationalists do not believe that the small nation-states can overcome global challenges by themselves. To fend off the neoliberal attack on social democracy, internationalists want to organise themselves on the same plane as global capital. Taken to its natural conclusion, this strategy turns the Europe of Nations into the cosmopolitan European Republic.

A Progressive Sense of Identity

Both strategies quickly reach their limits. Left-wing nationalism could certainly gain new supporters, but also risks alienating its own internationalist core members. On the other hand, the libertarian values of many internationalists are putting off the working class, whereas the equally cosmopolitan middle classes remain wary of redistribution.

Therefore, a successful strategy must think beyond the nation-state while also meeting people's needs for stability, security and belonging. That's why attempts to replace a cosmopolitan sense of identity with a more conservative position are proving futile. Replacing same-sex marriage and open borders with traditional family values and deportations doesn't work, and rather risks new divisions in the progressive camp. Ignoring basic emotional needs and focusing solely on material redistribution is equally misguided. Instead, a progressive concept of identity must link material distribution with cultural recognition.

Any attempt to construct a progressive sense of identity will inevitably face difficulties. Emotionally charged terms such as nation, patriotism and *Leitkultur* have no currency in the libertarian part of the social democratic sphere. Yet anemic concepts such as constitutional patriotism fail to meet human needs for belonging, pride, self-respect, honor, stability and security.

For Germans, the term *Heimat* (meaning "home" but also "sense of belonging") provides these emotional ties. Admittedly, it rouses mistrust in those who associate it with right-wing populist ideology. Yet this kind of essentialist interpretation plays straight into the hands of right-wing populists—they win the game without a proper contest. *Heimat* has no set meaning. Rather, it's meaning is determined by political struggles over its interpretation.

To be absolutely clear: a progressive interpretation of *Heimat* has nothing to do with chauvinism. This progressive understanding of the term needs to be internationalist and European. As such, the social-democratic *Heimat* is an open-minded place in the middle of Europe. But this can absolutely be combined with the vibrant culture of local traditions. Consequently, the reconstruction of communal spaces and shared symbols is an important part of this understanding of *Heimat*.

Heimat Is Living in a Good Society

Recently, there've been increasing attempts to set out a social democratic definition of *Heimat*. Too often, however, it's defined in cultural terms only. This inevitably results in conflicts between the cosmopolitan and communitarian lifeworlds of social democracy. Therefore, a social democratic definition of *Heimat* always needs a material counterpart: the progressive *Heimat* is a place where it's possible to live a good life in a good society.

A good society doesn't work without public services. If there are no buses or trains in rural areas, or if city streets are lined with litter, then a good life is more difficult. If young parents have to worry if they can afford a place in the nursery, or if women, gays and lesbians and refugees are too afraid to go out, society is not good.

The progressive Heimat constitutes a places and community that makes life worth living. It's rooted in local traditions and, at the same time, open to the world. The progressive *Heimat* helps people to shape their own lives and communities.

In rural areas as well as the "rust belts" of post-industrial cities, this means investing in mobility by expanding local public transportation, in basic infrastructure by providing postal services and fibre-optic broadband, in public amenities such as swimming pools and sports clubs, and in cultural facilities such as theatres and museums. It also requires a radical reform of the education system to meet the challenges of digitalisation. And the police and social security systems must be strengthened to overcome people's fears.

We can only achieve all of that through more financial resources for local authorities and regional governments. But the return of state investment requires an end to balanced-budget rules. In other words, the political goal of a livable *Heimat* is to free society from the neoliberal grip of austerity. After all, a state cannot perform the core function of social democracy—shaping society—if its hands are tied. A return to proper public investment provides social democracy again with its Keynesian tools. And social democracy will certainly need them to handle the crisis on the demand side that has been destabilising capitalism for decades.

The State and Europe

The commitment to Europe is not a purely rhetorical one, but indeed a substantial material offer. To strengthen Europe, France and Italy expect, for very good reasons, a clear sign from Berlin. However, it's hard to communicate demands for a transfer union in Germany. The end of austerity would open an escape route from this dead end of European politics. Overcoming the low investment rate in Germany would not only help the German economy, but also solve the euro crisis. The only meaningful signal to Germany's European partners would be alleviating the imbalances in Europe via more investments and increasing wages in Germany. The return of public services to the periphery signals to those who feel left behind that the state has not given up on them. Strengthening the welfare state as a bastion against the centrifugal forces of global financial capitalism helps to alleviate fears of downward mobility. Improved domestic security enables people to accept rapid changes in society. So a livable *Heimat* means control, and is therefore the best way to burst the bubble of right-wing populism.

In addition, a livable *Heimat* provides a shared platform where all strands of social democracy can find themselves represented. Strengthening domestic security is a key demand of the more conservative social democrats. The paradigm shift in economic and social policy is the main concern of the left. At the same time, the focus on state investment in public services is also attractive to those who are sceptical about redistribution.

To embed the issue of material distribution in a cultural framework is a winning formula that can work effectively in the emerging form of digital capitalism. Consequently, a livable *Heimat* is a first step in re-defining what social democracy means in the 21st century.

Behind the Progressive Discomfort with Nationalism

E. J. Dionne

E. J. Dionne is an influential scholar and political journalist based in Washington, DC. He writes a twice-weekly column for the Washington Post *and holds positions at Georgetown University, Harvard University, and the Brookings Institution.*

Most liberals have a problem with nationalism. John Judis has a problem with the problem liberals have with nationalism. This dynamic—or dialectic, if you prefer—makes Judis's latest book, *The Nationalist Revival*, essential reading. There are important lessons here for progressives. But there is also more to liberal unease with the new nationalism than Judis may acknowledge.

Through his long career in progressive journalism, Judis has made a habit of seeing things that others were missing. In the early 1990s, he took Ross Perot's movement seriously from the start. Through excellent reporting and listening, he came to understand the coherence of this middle-class, middle-of-the-road, and largely secular movement. He also saw early on how powerful a political issue opposition to free trade could become.

Judis offered a revelatory book in 2001 calling attention to the increasingly selfish and inward-looking nature of the American economic elite. *The Paradox of American Democracy* traced the transformation of the politics of business between the New Deal era and the end of the 20th century. From World War II through the late 1960s, Judis argued, significant parts of the business sector, while decidedly conservative, leaned more toward a middle-of-the-road, consensual approach to public life, reflected in the work of the Committee for Economic Development. Business leaders of

"Is There Such a Thing as Progressive Nationalism?" by E.J. Dionne, The American Prospect, April 1, 2019. Reprinted by permission.

this stripe supported moderate and even liberal Republicans and broadly accepted both Keynesian economics and the welfare state.

But during the 1970s, in reaction to growing foreign competition, the new consumer movement led by Ralph Nader, and the rise of new regulatory agencies (many of them, ironically, established during the Nixon administration), business shifted right. "[C]orporate leaders and bankers," Judis wrote, "abandoned their commitment to disinterested public service and to a politics that transcended class. They turned against union organizers, environmentalists and consumer activists with the same resolve that an older generation of business leaders had turned against the AFL, the IWW, and the Socialist Party."

It might be said that the perception of Washington as a "swamp" of special-interest groups took off in this period. Judis noted that the number of businesses with registered lobbyists in Washington rose from 175 in 1971 to 2,445 in 1982. The number of trade associations nearly doubled between 1978 and 1986, from 1,800 to 3,500.

Then came Judis's reporting over the last decade from Arizona and other states, which called attention to a burgeoning anti-immigration movement. Again, far earlier than most journalists, he saw how a backlash against migrants not only animated significant parts of the electorate but also spurred new forms of organizing on the right.

With his work on trade, elite behavior, and immigration, Judis might be said to have spent decades preparing himself for our current moment and developing the depth of understanding that allowed him to pack so much into his two compact and revelatory volumes for the impressive Columbia Global Reports series. His first, *The Populist Explosion*, provided one of the best early explanations for Donald Trump's victory—before Trump had actually won the election. It made an indispensable contribution to the debate over what populism is and isn't by pushing back against the idea that populism must necessarily be, as some scholars have argued, authoritarian and exclusionary. Rather, Judis saw populism more expansively, with both democratic and autocratic possibilities.

"It is not an ideology, but a political logic—a way of thinking about politics," he wrote. Populists wave warning flags that establishments are foolish to ignore: "They signal that the prevailing political ideology isn't working and needs repair, and the standard worldview is breaking down." That both the Bernie Sanders and Trump campaigns could be fairly called populist drove home Judis's central argument that populism existed on the left and the right (and, in the case of Perot, in the center, too). In Europe, France's far right National Front was populist, but so were Syriza in Greece and Podemos in Spain.

It was thus inevitable that Judis would turn his attention next to *The Nationalist Revival*. And nationalism is the harder challenge, intellectually, politically, and morally. If both populism and nationalism are contested concepts, nationalism arouses even more alarm—and loathing. Once again, Judis makes the case for conceptual nuance. Nationalism, he insists, "can be the basis of social generosity or of bigoted exclusion." It can be both "an essential ingredient of political democracies" and "the basis for fascist and authoritarian regimes."

Unlike many on the left, Judis has a long history of sympathy for nationalism. He wrote a manifesto for *The New Republic* in 1995 titled "For a New Nationalism" with Michael Lind, the brilliant and ideologically eclectic student of American nationalism and the contributions made by its advocates. Lind includes in their ranks Alexander Hamilton, John Quincy Adams, Abraham Lincoln, and Theodore Roosevelt (whose progressive 1912 program was also proudly touted as "The New Nationalism").

For Judis, a defense of nationalism is synonymous with a defense of a more egalitarian economy. The institutions necessary for greater economic justice, he argues, are under attack by globalization. He writes:

> The emergence of globalization in the 1970s has undermined the labor union and the locally owned factory and business

and the community they sustained. Finding themselves at the mercy of currency flows, footloose multinational corporations, and migrant flows, and afflicted by anomie and a sense of powerlessness—the individual has little recourse except the nation.

He goes on to use the everyday language of our politics to put nationalism in a sympathetic light. "Nationalism," he writes, "provides a framework within which citizens and their governments deliberate about what to do—and justify what they have done. Citizens debate whether a policy is in the 'national interest.'" Judis rightly points toward the prophetic and critical work of the economist Dani Rodrik on the paradoxes and costs of globalization. Had more attention been paid to Rodrik's warnings back in the 1990s about the political and social impositions of globalization, the nationalist backlash of our era might have been avoided—or, at the least, its most dangerous effects might have been mitigated.

One of Judis's conceptual contributions is to draw a sharp line between globalism, which he opposes, and internationalism, which he supports. Globalism, he says, "subordinates nations and national governments to market forces or to the priorities of multinational corporations." Internationalism, on the other hand, refers to the decision of nations to "cede part of their sovereignty to international and regional bodies to address problems they could not adequately address on their own."

It's a useful distinction that helps explain arguments within the British left over the decades about the European Union. Most left-wing opponents of the EU in Britain have always seen it as serving international capitalism. In Judis's terms, they saw it as globalism's agent. The majority of the British left (measured by opinion polling among the Labour Party's supporters) have come to see it instead as a classic case of internationalism, an effort to pool sovereignty for the purpose of empowering its members within the global system.

Many on the left will be receptive to Judis's focus on globalism, his discussion of the impact of trade on manufacturing jobs, and his argument that national sovereignty has been essential in the advancement of broadly social democratic policies. His insistence that national feeling has been central to the social solidarity that generous welfare states require is not a standard argument made by progressives, but it is important to ponder.

His is definitely not a book for those who argue that the proper location of solidarity is global and that it should reach all of humankind regardless of nationality. I don't say this to denigrate this generous side of cosmopolitanism. On the contrary, a strong case can be made from both religious and secular perspectives that more attention should be paid in our day-to-day politics to the poorest people in the poorest countries on earth. Yet I think Judis is right to call our attention to the need to pay far more attention than we do to those who typically pay the highest costs for globalization and technological change—the least advantaged classes in the wealthiest economies. Egalitarianism does begin at home, and economic justice within nations is a precondition to a sustainable politics of economic justice that stretches across borders.

After World War II, he writes, "the leaders of the victorious powers tried to prevent the revival of the toxic, aggressive nationalism that had arisen in Germany, Italy and Japan." The result? "In Europe and to some extent in the United States, the very term 'nationalism' and its cognates acquired a pejorative connotation. To call someone a 'nationalist' insinuated some underlying sympathy for Nazis or fascists."

Well, yes. For many on the left and center-left—I am among them—it is very hard to divorce nationalism from its murderous 1930s-1940s downside. In our book *One Nation After Trump*, my colleagues Norm Ornstein, Tom Mann, and I offered arguments that parallel Judis's in important ways. We agreed that progressives needed to acknowledge that democracy has largely prospered within nation-states and that the rise of nationalism in recent years was an expression of a desire by citizens to subject globalization to democratic discipline. We, too, cited Lind's work on the positive contributions of democratic nationalism in our history. And the very title of our book and its echo of the Pledge of Allegiance's commitment to "liberty and justice for all" reflected our view that progressive politics have always been linked to nation building rooted in social fairness and inclusion.

For this reason, we argued that progressives needed to embrace patriotism without shame or embarrassment. But we also sought to distinguish between patriotism and nationalism. We followed George Orwell, who saw patriotism as stemming from "devotion to a particular place and a particular way of life" while insisting that "nationalism, on the other hand, is inseparable from the desire for power." The 1930s experience really does make a difference. As Isaiah Berlin noted in the early 1970s, those who foresaw more benign forms of nationalism in the 19th century never contemplated "the pathological developments of nationalism in our own times."

"No one, as far as I know," Berlin continued, "had ever prophesied the rise of modern national narcissism: the self-adoration of peoples, of their conviction of their own immeasurable superiority to others and consequent right to domination over them."

Perhaps, as Judis and Lind might argue, the patriotism my colleagues and I recommended was not all that different from the democratic nationalism they endorse. We might be seen as making a distinction that is more sentimental than rigorous.

Yet I do not think it mere sentiment to challenge the idea that we can now safely ignore the toxicity that attached itself to nationalism in the decades after World War I. The right-wing ethno-nationalism of the Trump movement—visible in nationalist movements in Europe as well—draws on these older forms of fascism, sometimes explicitly, often implicitly. If this makes many on the liberal left nervous, well, it should.

This view has led some of Judis's critics to argue—Guardian columnist Jonathan Freedland's December review in The New York Times Book Review is thoughtfully representative—that he is too ready to adopt some of the anti-immigrant movement's language (about "a flood of refugees" and "a raging stream of migrants"). Freedland also noted that Judis's accounts of how the regimes of Orban's Hungary, Kaczynski's Poland, and Putin's Russia behave the way they do sometimes morphed from intelligent historical analysis into justification.

Freedland has a point on Hungary, Poland, and Russia. Judis clearly wanted to keep his book short, but he owed us more about the problematic nature of these regimes. He expresses proper discomfort with Orban's anti-Semitic campaign against George Soros, for example, but is too eager to criticize the European Union's pushback (an extremely mild pushback, it should be said) against the rise of authoritarianism in its ranks.

On immigration, the picture is more complicated. Judis is right to point out that we have had many earlier outbreaks of nativist feeling, and that the current backlash can be explained in part by the facts on the ground. There has been a sharp change in the ethnic composition of the pool of immigrants since the 1965 Immigration Act. And the proportion of our population that is foreign-born has risen dramatically, from 4.7 percent in 1970 to 13.7 percent today. Suggesting that it is not surprising that these factors have produced a reaction is not the same as justifying either racism or nativism. Nor is Judis wrong to argue that those of us who support relatively generous immigration policies need to think hard about the difficult compromises that might be required to rebuild a national consensus on behalf of the humane treatment of newcomers. Judis is sometimes too quick to rationalize the fears of the anti-immigration movement and to accept its faulty definitions of reality. There are times when he seems more morally offended by the obtuseness of cosmopolitans, the British author David Goodhart's "Anywheres," than by the rage of Goodhart's "Somewheres," those deeply attached to localities who are quite capable of their own old-fashioned prejudices.

Nonetheless, it is vital that progressives come to terms with what both of Judis's books have to teach. It is certainly a form of willful blindness to underplay the role of racism and prejudice in

Trump's campaign and to deny that racism and nativism motivated a substantial share of his supporters. But in political terms, the more costly mistake would be to assume that all of Trump's working-class voters were motivated by race alone and that they can therefore never be persuaded to an alternative politics.

The Democrats' 2018 successes in Pennsylvania, Michigan, and Wisconsin suggest that this pessimism is not justified by the electoral facts. And moving the country toward greater harmony (and, yes, justice) across the lines of race, ethnicity, and immigration status requires a new capacity for empathy toward those suffering from the costs of economic dislocation—in African American and Latino inner-city and rural neighborhoods and the old, predominantly white factory and mining towns alike. Judis may be a bit too grumpy about liberals. But his grouchiness should force liberals who live in prosperous precincts to ask themselves what role their indifference to the costs of the last two decades of economic change played in creating the mess we're in.

Nationalism Can Function in Support of a Democratic Political Culture

Marc Plattner

Marc Plattner is vice president of research and studies at the National Endowment for Democracy and founding editor of the Journal of Democracy. *His books include* Global Challenges to Liberal Democracy *and* The Global Resurgence of Democracy.

A recent article on the political situation in Europe by two European authors speaks of the EU as being "caught in the crossfire between nationalists and internationalists." And an American commentator, in an analysis of the upcoming presidential contest between Donald Trump and Hillary Clinton, has described the key political fault line separating the two candidates as "nationalism vs. globalism." Since Britain's vote to leave the EU, of course, discussion of nationalism has become even more prominent on both sides of the Atlantic.

I agree that a resurgence of nationalism is roiling the current politics of the Western democracies, but it is not always easy to identify the character of that nationalism. The term nationalism itself is a contested one, subject to different meanings and interpretations. The word, which was hardly used in English before the middle of the 19th century, is defined by the Oxford English Dictionary as "Advocacy of or support for the interests of one's own nation, especially to the exclusion or detriment of the interests of other nations." The clause following that word "especially" points to the reasons why there is disagreement not only about the meaning of nationalism but also about whether it is a good or bad thing.

"No nationalism, no democracy?" by Marc Plattner, Democracy Digest, August 2, 2016. Reprinted by permission. The article is based on the George Washington Memorial Lecture delivered by Marc Plattner, Editor of the Journal of Democracy, at the 2016 Estoril Political Forum on "Democracy and its Enemies: New Threats, New Possibilities." The lecture was originally published in the Portuguese journal, Nova Cidadania, Volume XVIII, No 60, Fall 2016, pp. 33-35.

The OED adds that while nationalism now "usually refers to a specific ideology," in earlier usage the term appears to have been "more or less interchangeable" with patriotism. Today patriotism certainly has a more positive connotation that nationalism, though it too is not without its opponents, who might be characterized as cosmopolitans. Or if one wanted to use more philosophic language to describe the dichotomy between nationalism and globalism or between patriotism and cosmopolitanism, one might speak of particularism vs. universalism.

In a brief but powerful essay published in 1990, the late Polish philosopher Leszek Kolakowski warned of the future dangers that "malignant nationalism" would pose for democracy. Nationalism is malignant, he contended, "when it asserts itself through belief in the natural superiority of one's own tribe and hatred of others; if it looks for pretexts . . . to expand into others' territories; and above all, if it implies an idolatrous belief in the absolute supremacy of national values when they clash with the rights of persons who make up this very nation." Yet Kolakowski also argues that "patriotic feelings are not in themselves incompatible with a democratic outlook, insofar as they mean a preferential solidarity with one's own nation, the attachment to national cultural heritage and language, and the desire to make one's nation better off and more civilized."

George Washington, of course, was famous above all as an exemplar of patriotism. His writings make it clear that he regarded duty and service to his country as his highest calling. He was often compared to the great Roman patriot Cincinnatus, who during a military emergency was chosen to be dictator for a six-month term, left his plow to command Rome's army, defeated the enemy, and within 15 days resigned and returned to his farm.

Yet although Washington was a patriot in the old Roman mode, he also was very much a man of the Enlightenment. He celebrated the fact that the birth of the American republic had occurred not "in the gloomy age of Ignorance and Superstition, but at an Epoch when the rights of mankind were better understood and more clearly defined, than at any former period." He emphasized the clearly defined, than at any former period." He emphasized the importance of scientific progress in supporting a political order founded upon liberty. In his First Annual Message to Congress in 1790, he told the assembled legislators: "[T]here is nothing which can better deserve your patronage than the promotion of science and literature. Knowledge is in every country the surest basis of public happiness." And he affirmed the universality of the principles underlying the American Revolution.

I would argue that there is no contradiction between Washington's Enlightenment-bred universalism and his deep-seated patriotism, but there is certainly a tension between them. Universalism or cosmopolitanism appeals to principles that apply equally to all human beings, regardless of where they live or the community to which they belong. Patriotism or nationalism, on the other hand, demands above all allegiance to one's own political community. There are obviously times and situations in which these two standpoints can come into conflict. And yet I would argue that reconciling them has been and remains essential to the healthy functioning of democracy.

Here the U.S. experience is particularly illuminating. This year marks the 240th anniversary of the signing of the Declaration of Independence, an event that Americans will celebrate as Independence Day a week from now. The Declaration is perhaps the first political document to justify the founding of a new polity on unambiguously universal principles, as its most famous lines make clear: "We hold these truths to be self-evident, that all men are created equal, that they are endowed by their Creator with certain unalienable rights, that among these are life, liberty, and the pursuit of happiness."

Abraham Lincoln would later call attention to this aspect of the Declaration by stating: "All honor to Jefferson–to the man who, in the concrete pressure of a struggle for national independence by a single people, had the coolness, forecast, and capacity to introduce into a merely revolutionary document, an abstract truth, applicable to all men and all times, and so embalm it there, that today, and in all coming days, it shall be a rebuke and a stumbling-block to the very harbingers of re-appearing tyranny and oppression."

As Lincoln's statement reminds us, however, the American Founders appealed to these universal principles in support not of a universal political goal but of a particular one—a struggle for "national independence" by Britain's North American colonies. The Declaration seeks to set forth and to justify a policy not of political union or integration but rather one of *separation*. Its opening paragraph invokes the necessity "for one people to dissolve the political bands which have connected them with another, and to assume among the powers of the earth, the separate and equal station to which the laws of nature and nature's God entitle them."

The Constitution of the United States, drafted and approved 11 years after the Declaration, also reflects the separateness of this "one people." As the Preamble states, it is "We the people of the United States" who establish this Constitution "in order to . . . secure the blessings of liberty to ourselves and our posterity." So while the American Founders believed that they were implementing universal principles that applied to and would appeal to all mankind, they saw this as perfectly compatible with establishing a political regime that would aim at securing the liberties not of all mankind but of its own citizens. Few would deny that governments—especially democratic governments—have a fundamental obligation to serve the interests of their own citizens. No one thinks it unreasonable for democratic political leaders to place the interests of their own country above those of other countries. Indeed, a president or prime minister who exposes his country's military forces to the risk of combat is expected to do so only if it promises to bring some larger benefits to his fellow citizens. And in a case where any of those citizens are in grave danger, such a leader would be regarded as derelict in his duty if he did not make the rescue of his fellow countrymen a much higher priority than that of other nationals.

The willingness to risk one's life on behalf of the political community to which one belongs remains a quality that is widely praised and admired. Patriotism is still generally considered a virtue. But does this mean that nationalism should also be considered virtuous? That of course depends on how the term nationalism is understood.

Nationalism clearly involves some kind of attachment to the nation, but the meaning of the word nation is itself ambiguous. For it can have both an ethnic and a political character. Moreover, for members of ethnic minority groups in heterogeneous societies these two meanings can be at odds with each other. A person's ethnic attachments may in some circumstances run counter to his political attachments, leading him to seek independence for his ethnic group rather than to support the larger political nation in which he lives. Catalan nationalists who seek independence or at least greater political autonomy for Catalonia are not considered Spanish nationalists.

By contrast, the term patriotism, as it is used in English at least, usually does not carry any ethnic overtones. It is most often defined simply as love for or devotion to one's country, and country is a word that describes the political community in its undivided totality.

How, then, should we understand nationalism's relationship to democracy? I certainly agree with Kolakowski that it can take malignant forms that put it at odds with democracy. A majoritarian nationalism that refuses to recognize the equal citizenship of members of ethnic minorities is incompatible with the equality before the law that is an essential element of democracy. At the same time, it is virtually inevitable that the culture of the majority, especially if it has a large numerical preponderance, will take precedence in areas such as language and education policy. A democratic country will show a decent respect for the culture and the rights of its minorities, but there is no feasible way to achieve perfect equality or fairness in these matters, and thus multiethnic societies will inevitably experience tensions and disputes over them.

So nationalism does pose threats to democracy, and these need to be met with prudent policies and practical compromises that will vary from country to country. But does nationalism also contribute in a positive way to democracy? Might it even be true that nationalism supplies something essential to democracy? I would ask you to consider the possibility that this may be the case.

In the early 1990s the *Journal of Democracy* published an article by the Georgian political scientist Ghia Nodia, entitled "Nationalism and Democracy" that I still consider one of the most insightful treatments of this complex and difficult question. Nodia's analysis was strongly influenced by his experience of the breakup of the Soviet Union, during which, in his words, "all real democratic movements (save the one in Russia proper) were at the same time nationalist."

Both movements for democracy and movements for independence, he argues, act "in the name of 'self-determination': 'We the People' (i.e., the nation) will decide our own fate . . . and we will allow nobody—whether absolute monarch, usurper, or foreign power—to rule us without our consent." Nonpopular forms of rule may be able to do without nationalism, but democracy cannot. Despite the dangers from its malignant forms, nationalism provides the cohesion that is necessary for a people to be able to govern itself.

What do these brief reflections suggest about the situation in which we currently find ourselves? There is no doubt that much of the nationalist resurgence we are witnessing today has an ugly aspect. But I think it would be a grave mistake to counter these tendencies by demonizing nationalism *tout court*. Indeed, I think one source of today's outbreak of ugly nationalism is that political and intellectual leaders have tended to give insufficient weight to popular feelings of patriotism and national pride. A democracy cannot be healthy if its citizens do not share such feelings, and concern with the excesses of malignant nationalism should not blind us to this fact.

Nationalism and the Politics of War

John Hutchinson

John Hutchinson is a professor in the department of government at the London School of Economics. He has written or edited over ten books on the subject of nationalism, including Nations as Zones of Conflict *(2005) and* Nationalism and War *(2017).*

Nationalism is often blamed for the devastating wars of the modern period, but is this fair? Critics pinpoint four dangerous aspects of nationalism: its utopian ideology (originating in the late 18th century), its cult of the war dead, the mass character of its wars, and its encouragement of the break-up of states. I argue, however, that the case against nationalism is not proven.

A first charge is that the ideology of nationalism is itself a cause of war. Nationalism is a secular "religion" that proclaims that the world is composed of unique and ancient nations which have exclusive homelands, and that the sacred duty of individuals is to defend the territory, independence, and identity of their nation. But critics say that nationalism is historical fantasy: such nations have not existed before the modern world, human populations more often than not have been intermingled, and attempts to separate them into exclusive territories generates conflict. Moreover, nationalists also deny all existing agreements, including treaties between states, that are not based on the free will of peoples. Nationalism thus necessarily leads to war. An awkward fact for this argument is that the number of interstate wars in the era of nationalism (the 19th and 20th centuries) has fallen. Many nationalisms are pragmatic and conservative in character. In fact, warfare was more frequent in the period before modern nationalism during the sixteenth and seventeenth centuries that

"Does nationalism cause war?" by John Hutchinson, Oxford University Press, February 4, 2018. Reprinted by permission.

were wracked by religious and imperial conflicts. The modern nation state system is arguably an effect of these wars.

A second accusation is that nationalism glorifies war through its cult of "fallen soldiers." The purpose of war commemorations, it is claimed, is to ensure a ready supply of recruits for future wars by appealing to the idealism as well as the "aggressive instincts" of young males. Some have even argued that "regular blood sacrifice" for the nation is necessary for social cohesion. To prevent social disunity, political leaders create external enemies, thereby diverting the violence inherent in human beings outwards rather than towards the powers that be.

But this is to simplify. While some politicians might evoke memories of "ancient hatreds" in their drive for power, remembrance ceremonies of the world wars, at least in Western Europe, are rather "sites of mourning" offering the lesson of "never again." The continued power of such ceremonies may be linked to the decline of traditional religions and the need to find a transcendent meaning for the tragedies of mass death. As George Mosse showed, nationalism took on the characteristics of a surrogate "religion," appropriating the iconography and even the liturgies of Christian religion during the 19th century, to extoll the fallen soldiers as national martyrs and make their military cemeteries, places of pilgrimage. Nationalists promise a kind of immortality to all who die for the nation in "being remembered for ever."

A third argument is that nationalist wars, if less frequent than those of the early modern period, are more destructive since nation states are based on a new contract between the state elites and the people. In return for citizenship, the masses agree to fight for the nation state. Before wars were fought largely by military professionals and for limited objectives, now they are peoples' wars conducted with unbridled passions. This began with the French Revolutionary period in the late 18th century and by the twentieth century wars became total, involving all the population. In the mechanised conflicts of industrialised nation states during the First and Second World Wars, civilians were as central to the war effort as the military and become targets. At its extreme, war can slide into genocide.

This third position too is one-sided. As states have been more representative of the people (more national), there has been a major shift in public spending from guns to butter. Today, at least in Western Europe, the welfare state has replaced the warfare state. Moreover, liberal nationalists and their nation states have been prominent in constructing international laws and bodies designed to regulate the conduct of war. These include Hague Peace Conferences, Geneva Conventions, the League of Nations, and the United Nations whose Charter narrowed the scope of legitimate war to that of self-defence. After the Second World War interstate wars between the great powers has declined steeply, in part because of this new internationalism.

Admittedly, violence within states (including civil wars) has increased since 1945, much of which arises from secessionist movements of minorities which claim the right to national self-determination. This can lead to state breakdowns and the creation of ungoverned spaces that become havens for global terrorist movements.

A fourth criticism, then, is that the principle of self-determination can lead to the break-up of states. This accusation too is overdrawn. The principle of self-determination by itself should not lead to state breakdown. States can offer federal and consociational (power-sharing as in Northern Ireland) arrangements, through which different national communities can be reconciled. Much of nationalist violence occurs in weak postcolonial states with multiple minorities that were rapidly constructed after Empires dissolved after 1945. It is the absence of unifying national loyalties that is the problem. Furthermore, the international peace-keeping missions formed to restore order in conflict zones are led by coalitions of nation states, often working under United Nations mandates.

To conclude, there are many varieties of nationalism, some xenophobic, others liberal-democratic and internationalist. Even the former is not necessarily a cause of war: other factors are usually required such as an external threat and a breakdown of the state. Indeed, where this occurs, the restoration of stability in the contemporary period is above all dependent on nation states acting in concert in the name of a ruled-based international order.

Nationalism and the Far Right

Daphne Halikiopoulou

Daphne Halikiopoulou is associate professor in comparative politics at the University of Reading. Her research has appeared in the European Journal of Political Research, *the* Journal of Common Market Studies, *the* Independent, Newsweek, *and the* Huffington Post.

Far right parties and groups have been enjoying increasing support across Europe. Such parties have performed well in recent domestic elections, often occupying second or third place – and in some cases joining governing coalitions. Examples include the French Front National (FN, now Rassemblement National), the Dutch Freedom Party (PVV), the Austrian Party for Freedom (FPÖ), the Norwegian Progress Party (FrP), the Italian Lega Nord (LN), the Sweden Democrats (SD) and Alternative for Germany (AfD).

Their shared focus on sovereignty, their scepticism of the EU, their emphasis on strict immigration policies and the placing of "native" inhabitants first in areas such as welfare and social services—policies that promote a "new nationalism"—have allowed researchers to compare these parties, often under the umbrella of the "far right."

However, the term "far right" tends to subsume a broad range of parties and groups that differ significantly in agenda and policy—especially economic and welfare policies—as well as the extent to which they support and employ violence. This category includes both parties that have moderated their agendas, distancing themselves from fascism in order to appeal to broader electorates; and vigilante street groups and extreme parties which employ violence, such as the Greek Golden Dawn

(GD), the English Defence League (EDL), Britain First and the Italian Casa Pound.

For this reason, the use of the term "far right" is often contested. So is it appropriate to group such different organisations under the same label?

Terminology

The short answer is "yes." Given the significant variations that exist between these parties and groups, any term that groups them together and compares them will have limitations. But the term "far right" is the least problematic precisely because it can be used, on the one hand, to identify the overarching similarities that make them comparable, and on the other to distinguish between different variants, allowing researchers to take into account the idiosyncrasies of specific cases.

The "far right" umbrella includes parties and groups that share an important commonality: they all justify a broad range of policy positions on socioeconomic issues on the basis of nationalism. The point here is not simply that they are all, to a degree, nationalist; but rather, that they use nationalism to justify their positions on *all* socioeconomic issues.

The term "right-wing populism," however, is less appropriate. Populism is an even broader umbrella that often includes disparate parties and groups. To narrow down this category, we often tend to conflate populism and nationalism, identifying a party as populist, not on the basis of its populist attributes—what party doesn't claim to speak on behalf of the people in a democracy?—but on the basis of its nationalist attributes. But despite the similarities between "populism" and "nationalism"—both emphasise conflict lines, focus on the collective, and put forward a vision of an ideal society—the two are conceptually different. While the former pits the people against the elites, the latter pits the in-group against the out-group.

And so herein lies the problem. If nationalism is always a feature of the far right, as most researchers agree, what is the added value of the term "populism"? To put it another way, what is the difference between a radical right-wing party and a populist radical right-wing party? While populism may or may not be an attribute of some far right parties, it is not their defining feature. Rather, nationalism is.

Extreme vs. Radical

Under the "far right" umbrella, we might distinguish between two sub-categories: extreme and radical right.

The extreme right includes both vigilante groups and political parties that are often openly racist, have clear ties to fascism and also employ violence and aggressive tactics. These groups may operate either outside or within the realm of electoral politics, or both. They tend to oppose procedural democracy.

The Greek Golden Dawn, for example, was formed as a violent grassroots movement by far right activists. Prior to its election to the Greek parliament in 2012, the party's main activities were confined to the streets. Researchers often label this party as fascist or neo-Nazi. Other examples include UK-based street movement Britain First, the English Defence League and its former leader Tommy Robinson. We might add various white supremacist organisations to this category, such as Stormfront in the US. It is notable that these groups often have ties between them—Stormfront, for example, often promotes Golden Dawn activities in its online materials.

The radical right tends to be the most widespread and electorally successful in Europe. These parties, which include the French FN (now Rassemblement National), Dutch PVV, Sweden Democrats, and the AfD, accept procedural democracy and have distanced themselves from fascism. They oppose the far right label.

These parties also use nationalism to justify all their policy positions. But instead of the ethnic nationalist narrative adopted by extreme right parties—which focuses on blood, creed and common descent—radical right parties utilise a civic nationalist narrative to promote anti-immigrant agendas, which allows them to appear legitimate to a broad section of the population.

This civic nationalist rhetoric presents culture as a value issue, justifying exclusion on purported threats posed by those who do not share "our" liberal democratic values. This strengthens the ability of these parties to mobilise on issues such as terrorism by linking anti-Muslim narratives to immigration and security. The justification is that certain cultures and religions are intolerant and inherently antithetical to democracy.

It also focuses on social welfare as an important aspect of the social contract between state and citizens. The positions of these parties are increasingly protectionist and welfare chauvinist, allowing them to mobilise the economically insecure by linking immigration, unemployment and (a purported) welfare scarcity.

This position is not incompatible with "far right" terminology. Extreme right variants have often been statist in their economic orientations—the classic example being fascism. Radical right variants, too, are increasingly departing from the neo-liberal economic formula of past years to adopt a more economically centrist position.

So, comparable does not mean identical. The BNP is not the same as UKIP. Similarly, Golden Dawn is not the same as the FN or the PVV or the AfD. But these groups are comparable; they all justify their policies on some form of exclusion of an out-group. Comparing them allows us not only to understand their different levels of success across Europe, but also the different forms they take depending on context and circumstance.

In northwest Europe, for example, the most successful far right parties are radical right variants that emphasise immigration and a cultural backlash, such as the PVV, the FN and the SVP; while in crisis-ridden southern Europe, successful far right parties, such as Golden Dawn, tend to be extreme variants which propose statist economic agendas.

But while these parties differ in many ways, their progressive entrenchment in their national political systems raises similar questions about out-group exclusion, anti-immigration narratives and mainstream responses. And this progressive entrenchment has comparable—and significant—implications for the nature of democracy and policymaking in Europe.

The Resurgent Dark Side of Nationalism

Prasenjit Duara

Prasenjit Duara is a professor in the department of history and East Asian studies at Duke University. He has written extensively on global politics and Chinese history and recently coedited A Companion to Global Historical Thought *(2014) with Viren Murthy and Andrew Sartori.*

Gunnar Myrdal is remembered for an expanded vision of development that accounted for institutions. Unfortunately, he also perpetuated a view that nationalism in Asia, fueled by ignorant and superstitious religiosity, was bad for development and that European nationalism was better: "In Europe, nationalism, despite its association with romanticism, remained secular and rational at its core." My view is that there is a more complex relationship between nationalism and economic development than Myrdal imagined—not just in Asia, but all over the world.

Nationalism Is a Complicated Relationship

Nationalism can be seen as a complex relationship and, like most such relationships, people have to work hard to balance the tension between *self* and *others*. While many nations have succeeded in using nationalism to develop, this same nationalism has also generated forms of exclusivism and competition that make it hard to resolve shared global problems. Economic development is an important—but not the only—goal that nations must pursue. While some see the rise of nationalism, or you might even say, *tribalism*, as a sign of the end of the world, there is actually a form of self-interest that has increased growth.

"Development and the crisis of global nationalism," by Prasenjit Duara, The Brookings Institution, October 4, 2018. Reprinted by permission.

Nationalism in Asia

Japan provides a surprising example. Meiji Japan's top-down nationalism led to rapid expansion of its own development as well as to imperial expansion. While the cruelties of Japanese colonialism have rightfully led to its denunciation, for various reasons, the institutions and programs established during Japan's rule in the colonies were well suited to modern development. After the war, countries such as Korea and Taiwan were able to adapt Japan's top-down model, its colonial institutions and a virulent anti-communist nationalism that—when combined with the security and economic opportunity by the United States—led to rapid growth. By the late 1970s, this exclusive form of nationalism was replaced in both countries by a grass-roots nationalism that demanded more participatory modes of political and economic governance, leading to more balanced growth.

Growth was likewise driven in the populous nation-states of China and India, despite their disparity in experiments with socialist forms of development and varied U.S. influence. Growth in both nations was enabled by powerful nationalist movements—especially revolutionary nationalism in China—premised on a more equitable contract with the population than the older imperialist order. Development, in other words, was encouraged by the inclusive nationalism that grew out of redistributive justice and the economic and political failures of the older system, and the rise of new classes that demanded change.

In Southeast Asia, the rise of the nation paired with inclusion (in a Japan-centered regional economy) led to growth during the 1970s-1990s. Interdependence was cemented after the Asian financial crisis of 1997-98 as the region emerged with new ideas for shared economic security through the Association of Southeast Asian Nations (ASEAN). While nationalist competition within ASEAN continues, it is still a major force for integration and growth.

The Two Forms of (European) Nationalism

The earliest forms of nationalism in Europe were closely linked to imperialism and the twin forces of economic development and exclusion, which continued well into the twentieth century. As Eric Hobsbawm has pointed out, imperial expansion was justified by a nationalism that was more racist than rational. Hannah Arendt points out that imperialists were able to harness nationalism because they claimed to supersede the reality of internal national divisiveness and represent the glory of the nation. Through the World Wars and on into the post-war peace, this "glory" has expressed itself in both hate and inclusion.

How can these impacts be so profoundly different? Scholars often distinguish between two types of nationalism: an *ethnic variety* built on race, religion, and language, versus a civic *nationalism*, in which rights are granted to all citizens, regardless of race, ethnicity, language, religion, or culture. German nationalism is, for example, often condemned as ethnic and exclusive, whereas Anglo-French nationalism is seen to be civic and inclusive. It is this the civic model that Myrdal had in mind when comparing Europe and South Asia, and it is this model that was dominant during the first few decades after the Second World War, embedded in the protocols of the United Nations and eventually leading to a notion of development that includes the eradication of poverty and higher standards of living for all.

Unfortunately, central to the modern history of nation-states is the alternation between capitalist expansion and a closing off of the national economy based on "the principle of social protection" but also on ethnic exclusivism and hostile nationalism. Today, aided by the volatility of the global economy, a narrower ethnic—sometimes even racist—vision of the nation has reasserted itself, which can be seen in the support of elected populist leaders around the globe.

It's the Movements that Count

These fluctuations in the tone of a particular form of nationalism are shaped by more than state-influenced macro-economic factors.

Most international studies of economic development take the nation-state as a stable basis of their analysis. When comparing the economic achievements or failures of nations, analysts refer to the state's aggregate indices and policies towards, say, capital formation, foreign debt, currency controls, or balance of trade. While indispensable, these analyses can miss how changes in *sociopolitical forces* transform development strategies and vice versa. Sociopolitical movements largely determine whether a nation turns inward or outward.

The imaginary—and the movements they often give birth to—can be integrative or contentious. To take the most evident expressions of how imaginaries have reshaped society and the world, consider the difference between Maoist and contemporary China or, for that matter, between Nehru's vision and contemporary India. While the broad goals of national development may remain, the frontiers of community inclusion, class configuration, and possibilities of nationalism have changed dramatically.

The U.N.-sanctioned civic model of nationalism and stabilization of economic flows (under the Bretton Woods regime of global economic exchange) produced the breathing space for emergent nations to cultivate inclusive national models of development. Many erstwhile colonies, which were multi-ethnic, embraced nationalist leaders who developed policies principally of civic nationalism to accommodate minorities.

In Asia, leaders such as Nehru and Sukarno of Indonesia and, later, Zhou Enlai of China, reiterated this commitment. They developed the principles of Panchasheela—a doctrine of non-interference in the internal affairs of others. Conflicts and pressures of the Cold War led to the movement's dissipation, but the civic inclusivism upon which they were cultivated has had an enduring influence in the larger nations of Asia.

Is This the End?

Nationalism in Europe and Asia has had many faces: revolutionary, top-down, anti-communist, participatory, civic, ethnic, and religious. The immediate post-war decades saw a largely inclusive civic model across much of the globe, permitting new nation-states to develop capabilities and resources without strong ethnocentric biases. The prevalence of the post-war inclusive model had much to do with the geopolitical circumstances of the victory of the Allied Forces in the Second World War, but it was also enabled by strong anti-imperialist national movements. They were also movements for the reduction of inequality and social justice.

More recently, the relationship between national political movements and economic development has taken a more sinister turn, exposing the tension between *self* and *other* that lies at the heart of all forms of nationalism. The global ascendance of neoliberal capitalism has been accompanied by the rise of chauvinistic, populist nationalism. The connection between nationalism and development appears to have come full cycle from a century ago, when its darkest forms drove the world into two global conflicts.

Have we learned the necessary lessons? On the one hand, nationalism today works to protect against real or perceived predation, as well as to integrate the nation for competitive advantage. On the other, while economic globalization has made the world more interdependent, nationalism has made it difficult to translate this interdependence into cooperation, especially for problems such as the planetary environmental crisis.

Nationalist Populist Movements Are a Shift Away from Global Liberalism

Aristotle Kallis

Aristotle Kallis is a British historian whose work focuses on modern European history with an emphasis on inter-war German and Italian fascism. He is a professor of history at Keele University in the United Kingdom.

After seemingly emerging strengthened from the First World War, liberalism suffered the political equivalent of near-death in the 1930s, attacked from illiberal and anti-liberal forces from left and right in large parts of the world. Against many odds, the period after 1945 gave liberalism a new lease of life. In spite of the division of the world into two ideological opposed camps, the liberal project flourished in "the west," gathered momentum post-1968, became a seemingly unassailable "regime of truth by the end of the century, and sought to become a universalisable paradigm of political order on a global scale. The dramatic events of 1989–1991 surrounding the collapse of the Soviet bloc and the end of the Cold War nurtured the illusion of a near-victory for this very liberal project on a near-global scale.

Since the turn of the new millennium, however, the illusion has started to turn into a nightmare. The rise of a multifaceted populist challenge to the liberal political mainstream exposed how shallow the supposed victory of liberalism was, even in its heartlands in Europe and North America. Exclusive nationalism and nativism, identity politics, critiques of globalisation and internationalism, increasingly bolder re-assertions of localised sovereignty—all increased their noise and mounted challenges that have tested the liberal reflexes and found them crumbling. Amidst this challenge, the project of liberal

"Populism, Sovereigntism, and the Unlikely Re-Emergence of the Territorial Nation-State," by Aristotle Kallis, Fudan Journal of the Humanities and Social Sciences, Springer Nature, May 30, 2018, https://link.springer.com/article/10.1007/s40647-018-0233-z. Licensed under CC BY 4.0 International.

universalism (in its various iterations as economic globalisation, universality of human rights, liberal internationalism, political federalism, cosmopolitanism, multiculturalism etc) came under sustained attack from a resurgent version of the paradigm of populist nation-statism. Sovereignty is at the very heart of this challenge; it is its primary justification, diagnosis, and roadmap of radical change for the future. "Taking back control" is the standard rallying cry on behalf of a radically re-defined community ("we"). It became the—very effective, as it turned out—rallying cry for the campaign to take the United Kingdom out of the European Union during the 2016 referendum. But I will argue that the very same call, in different discursive articulations, has become the critical common political denominator for all populist platforms and parties across Europe. In its own way, the vision has functioned as a powerful anti-utopia, a call to action in order to avert a perceived unfolding catastrophe, first, by projecting as a warning an extreme version of the present and, second, by offering an alternative path to a better future.

By all standards, "taking back control" is an evocative discursive construction. It projects agency and foreshadows the moral urgency of wholesale redress. It communicates a rupture with the present and posits a desirable future destination. It is anti-utopian in its critique of "the right to imperfection" and its associated rejection of a putative liberal universal "totality." But it is also pointing to the possibility of *eu*topia (a better alternative place) that is not just wishful thinking but possible and actionable. By "taking back control" one both actively prevents the unfolding of catastrophe *and* helps realise the normative claim of an allegedly better future. Thus, the critical tension between what 'is' and what "ought to be" is mediated by the dawning of a new radical potentiality—instead of what "should be" what "could be." "Taking back control" is the anti-utopian means to an end *and* the eutopian end itself; a kind of 'enacted utopia' that celebrates every small victory as the triumphant performance of the alternative future in the present; a realised counter-site, however small or partial, that underlines its difference from the other—still dominant—

liberal, internationalist, and globalising counter-spaces that it rejects and subverts.

The call to "take back control," whether articulated in these words or inferred from other related discursive formations, is simple and resonant. Nevertheless, its perceived simplicity belies a density of anti-utopian critique and counter-utopian proposition. Leaving aside for the moment the vision of "taking control," the formulation consists of four critical components—who must take control; *from who/where* this control should be wrested; *how* this control will be taken back; and *where* this control will be brought as a prized trophy. Theories on contemporary populism have answered convincingly the first three of these questions. According to the classic definition by Cas Mudde, populism is an ideology that considers society to be divided into two antagonistic groups, the homogeneous "people" and the corrupt "elite." In this bottom-up alternative vision to the current reality of establishment politics increasingly distant from the concerns of "real" people, populists argue that politics should be an expression of the general will of the people. It is this homogeneous "people" that is juxtaposed to the forces of internationalism, globalisation, and cultural diversity, which are articulated as direct threats to its existential security. This schema brings together a range of otherwise disparate targets—neo-liberal global elites and 'shadowy' transnational interests; the European Union in both its political and economic integrative functions; US economic, political, and military hegemony; immigration flows; and multiculturalism. Control, therefore, needs to be wrested from these sources of power through a number of strategies, including economic nationalism and an embrace of protectionism, political chauvinism, isolationism, reassertion of strict border controls, reversal of previous international commitments, and an expansive range of discriminatory measures targeting those excluded from the narrow definition of "the people."

It is the fourth component that interests me in this paper— the where to. I argue that populists have deployed an extreme concept of popular sovereignty—what Spiro, speaking in relation to the US context, referred to as "new sovereigntism"—in order to bestow intellectual coherence and communicative power to the disparate strands of their anti-utopian programmes. This political alliance between populism and sovereigntism has been articulated on the basis of *re-spatialising power*. The diagnosis is that such power has been slipping away for a long time, becoming more distant from the community and abused by external forces; but this process, it is argued, has now reached a tipping point, putting at direct risk the welfare of the community itself. Against the backdrop of a shrinking, diffuse, decentred, and unfamiliar world, where the infrastructure of globalisation is very much in place, the conventional political, cultural, social, and territorial entity of the nation-state becomes a legitimate and above all familiar and reassuring model to re-imagine and articulate this project of reclaiming sovereignty. Thus, the populist attack on the post-war globalising liberalism gives the traditional nation-state an unlikely new lease of life, in stark contrast to earlier confident prognoses that the era of the nation-state is drawing to a close. What is even more striking, I argue, is that nation-statism has become the locus of a convergence between populist platforms from both the right and the left. In arguing so, I do not seek to play down the significant intellectual differences between the two platforms (or indeed to apply the term "populism" uncritically to both). I do, however, seek to draw parallels in terms of their respective use of sovereignty as a discourse of popular mobilisation and to point out how otherwise very different claims for taking back control have resulted in a joint project to legitimise the re-concentration of power within the historic territorial contours and by the institutions of the nation-state.

Back to the Future: From Nation-Statism to Post-Sovereigntism…to Nation-Statism

Back in the heady days of the early 1990s, the Scottish professor of law Neil MacCormick made a passionate case against a sovereign-based legal and political international order. Viewed from a contemporary vantage point, the tone of his language underlines eloquently how the debate has shifted in the intervening quarter of a century:

> There is a widespread, but perhaps misguided, belief that there are a lot of sovereign states in the world, that this is a good thing … A different view would be that sovereignty and sovereign states, and the inexorable linkage of law with sovereignty and the state, have been but the passing phenomena of a few centuries, that their passing is by no means regrettable, and that current developments in Europe exhibit the possibility of going beyond all that. On this view, our passing beyond the sovereign state is to be considered a good thing, an entirely welcome development in the history of legal and political ideas.

The kind of de facto passing of the so-called Westphalian system of sovereign nation-states that MacCormick was celebrating in 1993 has been repeatedly proclaimed in the post-1945 period. Both *inter*national and *trans*national institutions and norms, it has been argued, have consistently eroded the sovereignty of traditional states—the majority of which have been constituted and behaved as nation-states. This is a process that is not unique to the post-World War II period. In fact, what modern political thinkers define as the "Westphalian system" corresponds only partly and imperfectly with the granular reality of politics and international relations in the past four centuries. As Krasner notes, the view that the erosion of traditional state sovereignty since 1945 is an exceptional trend is in itself "myopic." It assumes that there was a golden era of state sovereignty that puts the twentieth century at odds with the Westphalian model; and yet various levels and degrees of compromise and conflict, resulting in contestation, cession or loss of sovereignty, have marked the entire history of the sovereign nation-state. Nevertheless, it is possible to argue that the contradictions and flimsy assumptions of the Westphalian model have been unravelling faster and more extensively. Challenges have come from both outside the state (trans- and international) and inside it (sub-national). As a result, state sovereignty has been receding by choice and necessity alike.

On the one hand, nation-states have ceded voluntarily significant aspects—in varying degrees—of their sovereignty to a higher level of governance. On the other hand, the growing corpus of international obligations and the proliferation of transnational flows in the globalising world have de facto diluted or infringed on the norms of Westphalian sovereignty.

But does all this amount to a genuine post-Westphalian/ sovereigntist turn? In the last two decades of the twentieth century, a number of academics, politicians, and journalists wore their confident belief in the demise of the old Westphalian world on their sleeves. The growth of inter- and transnational trade; the dramatic proliferation of international organisations and of their ability to influence decisions; the exponential expansion of technological interconnectedness; all pointed, it seemed to them, to the dawn of a new epoch of globalisation that was disrupting beyond redress the traditional authority of the nation-state. Writing on the cusp of the new millennium, Elemer Hankiss discussed the globalisation-nation state dialectics and identified five main scenarios for the future. In four out of these scenarios, the power of the nation-state would suffer decline—a decline that ranged from outright implosion to transformation into an unrecognisable new political and social settlement, a "post-modern" nation-state. Only one scenario envisaged the strengthening of the power of the nation-state—and this would be only be in the direction of growing authoritarianism. Still, in all scenarios, the fate of the nation-state was directly linked to the dynamics and direction of globalisation, the latter being the major determining factor of the future international constellation. Tellingly, the 350th anniversary of the signing of the Treaty of Westphalia came and passed with little fanfare in 1998.

The prospect of a post-Westphalian future looks much less plausible from the vantage point of 2018. Since the turn of the millennium, a new era of sovereigntism has been predicated on the urgent need to reverse the trend of political and economic globalisation as inherently undemocratic and dangerous to the interests of the people. The confident predictions of the 1990s regarding the wholesale universalisation of the liberal settlement, let alone about its unabashed final victory at the end of the historical time, appear nothing less than hubristic today. It is supranational organisations and initiatives like the EU or the International Criminal Court, rather than nation-states, that now fight to shore up their political legitimacy against calls for scaling back or abandoning altogether the vision of global governance.

Still, on the eve of the hundredth anniversary of the end of World War I, one would be forgiven for confessing to a disquieting sense of déjà vu. Boyce has used historical analogy in order to stress that the world may have been in a not-too-dissimilar place before—a place where globalisation failed at the time of its seeming triumph, where liberalism imploded while apparently triumphant and approaching something akin the "end of history." After emerging from the First World War seemingly triumphant and on the road to a kind of an unprecedented kind of political hegemony, liberalism suffered the political equivalent of near-death in the 1930s, attacked from illiberal and anti-liberal forces from left and right in large parts of the world. Meanwhile what one may refer to as globalisation, already in motion since the early nineteenth century, gathered unprecedented pace in the 1920s only to plunge into a dual crisis of economic activity and political legitimacy in the 1930s. From the vantage point of 1939 and without the benefit of historical hindsight, liberalism seemed on its last leg, without much of a future beyond a few islands of exception. By contrast, nation-statism appeared on the cusp of re-defining the entire global political order. A utopian project at its core envisaging an ideal fusion between a strong, expanded state encompassing the entirety of a homogeneous national community, initially it took on a more pragmatic and moderate form as part of the post-1918 peace deliberations, in the form of national self-determination tempered by liberal guarantees for constitutional minority rights. However, a far more extreme, indeed chillingly utopian form of literal and aggressive nation-statism came to the fore in the 1920s and vied for supremacy in the 1930s—and did so largely by taking advantage of liberal inaction in the face of a crisis that turned the presumed certainties of the post-WW1 world upside down. Liberal elites held an exaggerated view about the resilience of the global(ising) order that they presided over post-1918, under-estimated the extent of the anti-liberal challenge from different sides, and over-estimated (in some cases massively) the degree of popular support that existed even in core constituencies for their brand of brave political and economic new world. Fascism found in nation-statism a utopian project that ticked the primary boxes of strong and authoritarian government, organic national unity, and aggressive, uncompromising pruning of the national community from foes, threats, and alien elements.

Against many odds, 1945 marked the collapse of fascism as a mainstream political project. The period after 1945 gave the gasping liberalism of the interwar years a surprising new lease of life, a second or indeed unlikely third chance after the setbacks of the two world wars. In spite of the division of the world into two ideologically opposed camps, the liberal project flourished in "the west" and sought to become a universalisable paradigm of political change on a global scale. [...] Saskia Sassen painted a mixed picture as an alternative to the simplistic zero-sum confrontation between internationalism and nationalism. She did argue that "sovereignty has been decentred and territory partly denationalized"; but she also added an important caveat:

> Sovereignty remains a feature of the system, but it is now located in a multiplicity of institutional arenas: the new emergent transnational private legal regimes, new supranational organizations (such as the WTO and the institutions of the European Union), and the various international human rights codes. All these institutions constrain the autonomy of national states; states operating under the rule of law are caught in a web of obligations they cannot disregard easily. ... What I see is the beginning of an unbundling of sovereignty as we have known it for many centuries. ... But it seems to me that rather

than sovereignty eroding as a consequence of globalization and supranational organizations, it is being transformed.

It could also be argued that the political and institutional parabola of what is now known as the European Union has ventured further and more swiftly than any other post-war institution from conventional understandings of national sovereignty. The combination of political expansion, socio-economic integration, institutional elaboration, and removal of boundaries in key areas from trade to currency exchanges to citizen migration challenged many of the assumptions about the ineliminable core of nation-state sovereignty and the existence of a bounded political community at its very heart. Giving up such powers originally rooted in the very exercise of sovereignty was—and remains—a voluntary act decided by the nation-states as government and people. The entire discourse of "post-sovereignty" has drawn most of its legitimacy by precisely anticipating its fiercest critique—the resulting *loss of sovereignty and the possibility that this outcome was an irreversible one. It was at this point that the argument of pooling sovereignty struck deliberately at the heart of the 'zero-sum' logic of the sovereign pool. Simply put, it was not argued that pooled sovereignty is a variable-sum game with a positive balance sheet, whereby one's perceived loss is no competitor's equivalent gain or indeed may produce multiple gains in power and prosperity for all.* MacCormick recast the link between sovereignty and the modern state with a help of a memorable analogy:

> Where at some time past there were, or may have been, sovereign states, there has now been a pooling or a fusion within the communitarian normative order of some of the states' powers of legislation, adjudication and implementation of law in relation to a wide but restricted range of subjects. … We must not envisage sovereignty as the object of some kind of zero sum game, such that the moment X loses it Y necessarily has it. Let us think of it rather more as of virginity, which can in at least some circumstances be lost to the general satisfaction without anybody else gaining it.

The critique of conventional understandings of sovereignty, first, as fixed on a bounded (national) territory and, second, as a finite, "zero-sum" entity challenged the assumed conceptual dependence of sovereignty and the territory of the modern nation-state. This is not to question in the slightest that the success and resilience of sovereignty as a principle of the modern state system owes a crucial lot to its territorial underpinnings; but it does reflect the Zeitgeist of the 1990s—a confident conviction that the growing gap between juridical (de iure) and new forms of effective (de facto) sovereignty had rendered traditional understandings of territoriality and power unfit for a globalised world. From economic flows to legal and judicial pluralism, from mass migration movements to security threats, from disruptive forms of knowledge economy to plural citizenships, the notion of a territorially bounded exercise of sovereignty was found to be inadequate. In the face of all these and other challenges to its territorial constitution, the contemporary state is not necessarily less powerful—but it is significantly less sovereign in effect.

Populism and Sovereigntism

At the heyday of the liberal confidence in globalisation's irreversible forward March, Dani Rodrik struck a discordant note when he spoke of the danger that this same globalisation was advancing much faster than our ability to govern it or indeed our capacity to comprehend it; and this situation was likely to generate a backlash against it.[1] Hans-Georg Betz spoke of the "new politics of resentment" when he accounted for the early signs of a radical right-wing electoral resurgence in the early 1990s amidst an atmosphere of growing insecurity and fluidity. The intensity and magnitude of the challenge may not have been clearly evident then but the key ingredients of a backlash were very much in place long before the 2008 global financial crisis—a perception that too much national control had been ceded to distant or diffuse centres of power; that political decisions made by governments no longer represented the interests of the people; and that, because of the above, governments appeared increasingly incapable of fostering security and identity when this was most needed. As Wallace noted with regard to the EU in 1999, while most of the "substance of European state sovereignty has now fallen away, the symbols, the sense of national solidarity, the focus for political representation and accountability, nevertheless remain." The tentative prediction offered by Rodrik—that "the government would come under severe pressure from workers to restrict international economic integration"—could easily be translated in the field of governance too. With the benefit of just enough hindsight, he argued in 2011 that it had become practically impossible to pursue at the same time democracy, a strict definition of sovereignty, and unfettered globalisation.

Within only a few years, it would seem, the world moved incongruously from a globalisation Zeitgeist to a nationalist-populist one. The orthodoxies underpinning the confident belief in the seemingly unstoppable forward drive of globalisation and internationalism started giving way to doubts, then to panic reactions, and finally to antagonistic "zero-sum" alternative perspectives that entered the political and social mainstream with striking ease. In his historical survey of the concept of sovereignty, Hinsley found that articulations of sovereignty tend to be more pronounced and widespread when "conditions have been producing rapid changes in the scope of government or in the nature of society or in both." I would argue that this observation is more relevant to *perceptions* of effective sovereignty rather than to the actual legal constitution thereof. As early as 1960, Elmer E. Schattschneider analysed how ordinary people find themselves increasingly cut off from influencing democratic decision-making—by all accounts one of the most foundations of modern democratic politics—and have thus been reduced to a 'semi-sovereign' status. This trend of sovereignty slipping away from democratic polity, as Mair (has argued, is now reaching the point of transforming the people into a "non-sovereign" actor.

It is precisely from the launchpad of democratic self-determination that contemporary populists have attacked the rapid growth of inter- and transnational channels that has been the hallmark of globalisation. Populism has emerged as an increasingly powerful and attractive political bulwark and redress to liberal democracy and globalisation. As a discourse, it is centred on an understanding of politics as an antagonistic relationship between "the people" and "the (power-wielding but inherently perceived as illegitimate and unaccountable) elite." The jury may still be out on the question of whether this understanding of populism qualifies it as an ideology in its own right, even a "thin-centred" one. For the purpose of my analysis, I approach populism as both a "political *strategy* of exercising power based on direct, unmediated ... support from ... largely unorganised followers"; and a discursive *filter* akin to a schema that recasts conventional, often antinomic political problems and goals in a more way that resonates to contemporary audiences.

It is on this basis that I seek to understand the contemporary populist challenge as closely coupled with a new form of sovereigntism that traverses conventional political divides and extends beyond the critique of any particular sphere or institution. Strictly speaking, the two components of this composite phenomenon have their separate conceptual and political histories; but taken together they represent a significant amplification of the sovereigntist discourse that is both quantitative and qualitative. While in quantitative terms it represents a dramatic intensification of the attack on the legitimacy of political, economic, and cultural globalisation as an elite-driven project, in qualitative terms it amounts to a recasting of this project as a composite threat to the security and prosperity of "the people" and posits a credible and actionable alternative vision of governance. The associated hardening of the "zero-sum" perspective on sovereignty that has been the node of contemporary populist discourses across the world underlines the necessity of not just arresting the process of transfer of power away from the territorial state but of reversing the flow altogether.

But is this particular understanding of sovereigntism robust enough in conceptual terms to overcome conventional divides between right and left, "exclusive" (that is, predominantly identitarian) and "inclusive"(that is pluralist and socio-economically driven) populism? Writing about the rise of SYRIZA in crisis-hit Greece, Stavrakakis and Katsambekis have turned the question on its head, arguing that, while so-called contemporary "inclusive" alternatives to liberal democracy observed in Latin America and southern Europe may be fruitfully analysed as "populist," the term may not be appropriate for the "exclusionary," hyper-nationalist and even racist discourses emanating from the radical right. This and other similar critiques of the semantic conflation of right- and left-wing operationalisations of "the people" into a single "populist" label have evinced an objection to treating the common component—the invocation of "the people"—in isolation from its perceived "other"—elites versus under-privileged, such as immigrants, refugees etc. For this reason, I wish to proffer sovereigntism and the re-territorialisation of state power that it effectively promotes as a potential way out of this methodological cul-de-sac. But in order to articulate what is genuinely new about the contemporary coupling of populism and sovereigntism, I wish to focus less on the actual legal dimensions of sovereign power than on the locus of the *performance* of sovereignty. Staging emotive spectacles of reclaimed sovereign power is an essential facet of the populist strategy that seeks to juxtapose such performances of a re-empowered demos to the alternative of a profound systemic crisis that threatened the very security and welfare of the people. In this respect, any project that seeks the re-territorialisation of power as an antidote to a perceived crisis point derived from decades of outflows to ever-distant, unaccountable or unrepresentative global centres must draw a new line of defence; a line that both continues to underline the danger "outside" and celebrates the reconstitution of popular sovereignty "inside."

The Border as the Locus of the Populist Performance of "Taking Back Control"

We have thus reached the border, the most tangible and symbolic marker of sovereignty in the history of the modern state. The border is a central component of the operation of sovereignty in international law since it is through it that the territory of one state (and thus its legal jurisdiction) is separated from another. This border, the theatre of the most brutal episodes in recent and distant history, the locus of traditional conceptions of sovereignty from Jean Bodin and Thomas Hobbes to Carl Schmitt, the border that according to globalisation theorists only two decades ago was becoming porous, waning or disappearing altogether as a temporary phase in the history of sovereignty, that same border is being re-constituted as a place of physical and figurative action. In historical terms, borders have served a number of practical purposes on behalf of the nation-state. I will single out four: giving a sense of exclusive, secure space to the community of citizens inside; creating a delineated territorial and political sphere that roots and protects the right to popular self-determination; marking the geographic contours of cultural and historic identities that were at the heart of the bounded community that they enclosed in opposition to surrounding "others"; and controlling movements in and out of the bounded state. In all these functions, the state border is a marker that is both physical and symbolic, inclusionary and exclusionary.

The paradox of the border in the contemporary globalised world is that its symbolic significance as the locus of performing sovereignty has increased exponentially at the same time that the state's ability to supervise it as the marker of its full de lure jurisdiction has declined markedly. The sovereigntists of the populist radical right have come to view it as a bulwark of a nativist, homogeneous community against incursions from people, ideas, commodities, and any other flow from the perceived 'outside' that could threaten the identity and welfare of the bounded community. Their conception of sovereignty is inextricably linked with the physical, legal, and symbolic performance of sovereignty at the border, the point where full bio-political control can be enacted over the bodies of those arriving; and where the full spectacle of legal and political self-determination can be performed vis-a-vis the outside world. It is of course far from coincidence that during the campaign for the referendum on the British membership of the EU, the Leave campaign used the imagery of the border as the most eloquent marker of the difference between in and out, between a crisis-ridden present and an alternative future of re-territorialised popular self-determination: on the one hand, there was the prospect of reinstating full sovereign control over national borders, the promise to substantially cut migration, and the prospect of clawing back powers that would belong exclusively to the UK Parliament; on the other hand, there was Brussels—a distant city, capital of another state, seat of a powerful, elitist international organisation, synonym of a federalist bureaucracy that was the exact opposite of what the sovereigntist nation-statism stood for.

The "border sovereignty" obsession of the contemporary populist radical right with immigration has of course its roots in the recasting of a "post-fascist" right that has unfolded since the 1960s. Ethnopluralism became the ideological fodder for reconstituting national state borders as absolute markers of bounded homogeneous nativist communities against the threat of ever-"softer" borders caused by globalisation, political integration, and the widening of the scope of international human rights law. Ethnopluralism stated a belief in the difference (but crucially not biological or cultural inferiority) and the incompatibility between different groups. In so doing, it also recast the idea of exclusive, *territorially bounded* communities for a formally post-racial world while continuing to emphasise the critical significance of the state border as the defender of unique characteristics of the community residing in it.

Precisely because the populist radical right has made such an investment in an extreme zero-sum sovereigntist formula, it is not just sovereignty itself but also its panegyric redemption from the grip of the international/globalised agents that needs to be performed. This performance can take a number of forms, ranging from reinstating hard borders to revoking visa stipulations to enhanced policing and militarisation of the border itself to the threat of deportation to the literalisation of the state border as the marker of a bounded community by building a wall. At a time when walls and fences proliferate across the globe as last-ditch defences against unpredictable migration flows, as they enact extreme security regimes on the literal and symbolic cusp between "the people" and the rest, they also perform chimeric tales of nation-state sovereignty as compensation for the increasing inability (or indeed failure) of the Westphalian state to deal effectively with the globalising, trans- and international trends. They turn borders into theatres of performing resistance to the—branded as illegitimate and undemocratic—diktats of global governance.

The ongoing conflict between the EU and particular member-state governments about the fate of refugees inside the Schengen Area of the union is indicative of both the real and the symbolic performance of sovereignty at the (internal) border. In the midst of the 2015 refugee crisis, the Hungarian government decided to erect a long 'border barrier' along the country's frontier with Serbia and Croatia. While the barrier proved effective in halting the refugee flows into Hungary and diverting them to other parts of the continents, it also staged a theatrical performance of sovereignty as permanent security "reassurance" to the Hungarian citizens, with a conspicuous consumption of hi-tech policing and surveillance technologies. Meanwhile, in spite of a ruling by the European Court of Justice calling on the Hungarian and Slovak governments to implement the 2015 quota agreement for the relocation of refugees inside the Schengen Area,[2] the Hungarian PM Viktor Orban has refused to implement it, citing security and identity concerns in relation to the refugees.[3] Thus, notwithstanding threats from the European Commission to sue the two member-state governments, Hungary has successfully defied its international commitments as a member of the EU and has staged an ever-more permissive festival of sovereign authority centred on its border in the buildup to the 8 April 2018 parliamentary elections.[4] The border barrier both marked the stage of a complex sovereignty competition between the transnational and the national; and indexed a convincing repatriation of sovereign power by the re-territorialised nation-state. Empowered by the result of a 2016 referendum on the quota obligations that, albeit recording a record-low turnout of just under 40% and thus declared void, returned a 98% support for the government's intransigent position,[5] Orban could effectively claim that he was clawing back sovereign control from distant or invisible elites on behalf of the Hungarian and indeed European people.

The strategy has paid off, as evidenced by the electoral triumph of Fidesz in the 2018 elections (49.27% of the vote and 2/3rds majority in the parliament). It is no coincidence that the most effective discourse employed by the Leave campaign during the 2016 EU referendum in the UK focused on the reconstitution of a 'hard' border in relation to immigration and free movement of workers from and to the EU. But it is also true that the "border sovereignty" platform pursued by the Leave campaign cut across traditional party and ideological lines by also invoking another performance of sovereignty—what has been generally referred to as "domestic sovereignty," namely the primary power of the legislative and executive institutions of the state to decide and implement policies within its borders on behalf of its citizens. The power of popular sovereignty's democratic appeal to "the people," to the majority of the people as expressed through public debate, voting in elections or in some cases participating in referendums, has been identified as being in a tense relationship with liberalism's emphasis on individual freedoms and constitutional restraints on majority rule. Populists have invested their appeal to "the people" with a powerful claim to seek a corrective to the alleged elitist distortion of or disregard for popular will. Against the backdrop of a crisis of popular representation and legitimacy in contemporary liberal democracy, domestic sovereigntists seek to redeem power on behalf of the previously marginalised majority and the privileged elite minority.

It is when we talk about this "democratic"/"domestic" dimension of the contemporary populist sovereigntist discourse that boundaries between ideologies and sites of performance of sovereignty become increasingly blurred. A lot has been said and written about the similarities and differences between the so-called populism of the right and the populism of the left. Mouffe has argued that the political right enjoys no monopoly on populism and that a left-wing populism is possible and is needed urgently in these anti-democratic times. Étienne Balibar has called for a progressive antidote, inspiring and popular enough to weaken the current appeal of exclusive hyper-nationalist and often racist populism of the radical right; in essence, he has sung the praises of a positive populism that sees in the redemption of popular sovereignty the end to the disempowerment of the people by unaccountable regimes. It would of course be heuristically unhelpful to simply conflate these rather different counter-propositions that derive from anti-diametrical views on the membership of "the people" and the modalities of power reclaimed on its behalf. Nevertheless, in heeding Balibar's call to develop an inspiring counter-populism that addresses popular frustrations but channels them into inspiring progressive action and the reclaims the discursive terrain of sovereignty from the far-right, democratic sovereigntists of the left have ended up injecting legitimacy to the old project of re-territorialising the power of the nation-state.

Much that Balibar has evangelised a transnational framework for his positive and emancipatory left-wing populism, the borders of existing nation-states have become an unlikely meeting point between the two competing populist projects. While one side sees the border in terms of defence against the corroding effects of neo-liberal economics, right-wing populists embrace it as the absolute filter of the future membership of the bounded (national) community. For democratic sovereigntist movements like Podemos in Spain, clawing political control back to the level of the nation-state may be more accurately explained as an interim strategy of reversing disempowerment in favour of an emancipatory and inclusive political vision of popular sovereignty. By contrast, the populist sovereigntism of radical right-wing movements like the Front National or the Party for Freedom (PVV) in The Netherlands aspires to the reterritorialisation of sovereign power and the exclusive redefinition of a homogeneous people as the endpoint of a counter-utopian vision. Still, however different their performances of sovereignty, the two projects converge on the reinvention of the border—symbolic and physical—of the existing nation-states as the marker of redeemed sovereignty. For the left-wing sovereigntists, the road to the constitution of the desired transnational demos may prove longer, more copious and twisted than originally expected. In the meantime, the re-territorialised sovereignty of the nation-state may prove a cogent, highly attractive, and thus resilient common denominator for sovereigntists across the ideological divide, just like nationalism had always lay at various critical intersections of left- and right-wing projects of Euro-scepticism.

Conclusions

Between critiques of globalisation and internationalism, of transnational or supranational or even federal reconfigurations of power and of eroded identities, the territorial nation-state has somehow managed to emerge as the unlikely survivor of the backlash against the post-war liberal global order. Sovereigntism—the belief in the uncontested primacy of national-level politics and the call to recover *at this precise level* (institutionally as well as territorially) power that has slipped away to more distant and diffuse layers of governance—has emerged as one of the primary ideological-political fault lines of contemporary politics, cutting across conventional left–right divides. This sovereigntist perspective is the primary beneficiary of a multifaceted populist critique of globalisation and the demise of the premise of "post-sovereignty" that was so in vogue only two decades ago. It is benefitting from lying at the point of intersection between rival populist projects of re-defining and allegedly re-empowering the community of "the people" against distant, detached or unaccountable elites. It is also benefitting from a strong preference for reconceptualising sovereign power along defensive territorial lines, clawing back control behind recognisable frontiers of existing states, on behalf of popular communities residing within the contours of established nation-states. Of course differences between left- and right-wing populist sovereigntist projects are too important not to mention—differences in the definition and scope of "the people," in the character of "the elites" that are targeted, and in the desired effects of the recovered power. Furthermore, for right-wing populists the re-territorialised sovereignty of the nation-state is the ideologically desired endpoint of their angry politics of backlash, while for their left-wing counterparts it is at best an interim position of pragmatic retrenchment en route to a favoured transnational redefinition of the re-empowered demos. Nevertheless, in the short term the two populist projects have sought to stage their performances of sovereigntist redemption on, behind or inside the borders of the nation-states. In their different ways, the reinstatement of hard borders against refugees and immigrants, the "taking back control" from international or supranational institutions in the name of empowering the demos, the targeting of diverse "out-groups" in the context of a zero-sum competition for power—all preface a plagiarised spectacle of territorial sovereignty that exudes angst, disorientation, and an exhausted political imaginary typical of an uncertain interregnum.

Notes

1. See also Saval (2017) 'Globalisation: the rise and fall of an idea that swept the world,' *The Guardian*, 14 July. http://www.theguardian.com/world/2017/jul/14/globalisation-the-rise-and-fall-of-an-idea-that-swept-the-world.

2. Byrne, Andrew. "EU's Top Court Dismisses Hungary and Slovakia Refugee Complaint." Financial Times, September 6, 2017. https://www.ft.com/content/9116ebbc-92de-11e7-bdfa-eda243196c2c.

3. Byrne, Andrew, and Neil Buckley. "Hungary Defies German Call to Accept EU Refugee Ruling." Financial Times, September 13, 2017. https://www.ft.com/content/0396b866-9811-11e7-b83c-9588e51488a0. 4. "Hungary Builds New High-Tech Border Fence—with Few Migrants in Sight." *Reuters*, March 2, 2017. https://www.reuters.com/article/us-europe-migrants-hungary-fence/hungary-builds-new-high-tech-border-fence-with-few-migrants-in-sight-idUSKBN1692MH.

5. "What Does Hungary's Migrant Quotas Referendum Mean for Europe?, Human Rights Watch, October 6, 2016. https://www.hrw.org/news/2016/10/06/what-does-hungarys-migrant-quotas-referendum-mean-europe (Accessed 26 February 2018).

CHAPTER 2

Is There a Difference Between Nationalism, Nativism, and Patriotism?

Populism and Nationalism in Modern World History

Peter Wilkin

Peter Wilkin is divisional lead in the department of communications, media, and cultural studies at Brunel University in London. His written work has appeared in Third World Quarterly, *the* British Journal of Politics and International Relations, *and the* European Journal of International Relations.

The resurgence of populist social movements around the world-system has been interpreted in a number of ways. For some it is a reassertion of the rights of sovereignty for political communities seeking to defend the nation-state from globalization, while others see it as reflecting a breakdown in the existing political order and a challenge to liberal democracy. There is an extensive debate on the political left regarding the extent to which populism can ever be a force for progressive social change.

What is clear, however, is that there is little consensus as to the meaning of populism, other than broad brush strokes and the idea that populism means *the people*. It is hard to imagine a populism that did not, in some sense, appeal to the people. The questions here are: which people, and how is this to be determined?

The grounds on which appeals to the people are made vary, from ethnic nationalism to support for universal human rights. Critics have often viewed populism as an expression of the irrational in politics, perhaps of an unruly mass threatening civilisation through aggressive and undemocratic actions. Anne Applebaum made this point about the Seattle World Trade Organisation protests in 1999 when she asked, "who elected the anti-capitalist convergence?" A number of factors tend to recur

"Rip It Up and Start Again: Populisms in the World-System," by Peter Wilkin, Journal of World-Systems Research 24(2):314-324 (2018). DOI 10.5195/JWSR.2018.855, University of Pittsburgh, https://jwsr.pitt.edu/ojs/index.php/jwsr/article/view/855. Licensed under

when definitions of populism are put forward and they can be succinctly dealt with here:

- Populism is the people, usually juxtaposed with the elites. The latter are viewed as being corrupt, Machiavellian, amoral and out of touch with the people.
- Populism is lacking in reason or prone to irrational demands; populist movements fail to understand the nature of political compromise and lack the maturity of conventional political parties and processes as is needed for liberal democratic electoral politics to function.
- Populism is often associated with demagogic or charismatic individuals and leaders who have an unnerving capacity to rouse emotions and mobilise anger.
- In the current era, populism is closely linked with illiberalism, by which is meant a fundamental challenge to important liberal principles, such as the rule of law, individual liberty, human rights and meaningful democratic elections.
- Populism in its extreme form threatens liberal democracy in the name of a utopian vision.
- For many critics, populism is often associated with a conspiratorial view of politics, which might manifest itself in critiques of the mass media as being a tool of powerful interests or of conspiracies organized by elites.

While populist movements are also social movements that seek to mobilise the people, it is less clear-cut that all social movements are populist. As Roberts and others have noted, the relationship between the two concepts has tended to be under-examined in academic literature, but it is an important one.

In the context of the evolution of the modern world-system (MWS), a key issue to consider is the extent to which populist movements can be viewed as being anti-systemic. If we accept that anti-systemic movements can be progressive *or* reactionary in their goals and outlooks, then the label anti-systemic is appropriate. By progressive I mean that the goals are broadly ones that promote universality in the form of a general improvement in the quality of people's lives. A good example of this can be found in the United Nations Sustainable Development Goals agreed upon in 2015.[1] Progressivism has its intellectual antecedents in the legacy of Enlightenment thought. By reactionary I mean the tradition that emerged as the Anti-Enlightenment, which sought to promote the ideas of separation, particularism and ultimately ethno-nationalism as the basis for a social order and a political system. Both kinds of populist social movement can be seen as being anti-systemic in ways that might transform the world-system.

Populism in the Modern World-System

By the end of the 1980s a decisive shift in the balance of power in the MWS occurred with the collapse of the Soviet system and the formal end of the Cold War. Structurally the Cold War had locked in place a geo-political order with two "spheres of influence" (generally seen as East-West, but in world-system terms more usefully viewed as a conflict between the core and parts of the semi-periphery), enabling governing client regimes to use various forms of coercion, bribery, co-optation, intimidation and violence to quell nascent protest movements and maintain civil order as best as possible.

The end of the Cold War also brought with it an opening in terms of political space, which enabled pronounced shifts in the nature of the political order across many parts of the semi-periphery. The spread of often very fragile forms of democracy, from South Korea through to Brazil, meant that previous forms of state violence against social protest became more problematic, though not impossible.[2] Crucially it needs to be borne in mind that democracy in the semi-periphery has been built on the foundations of highly authoritarian systems. Many of the actors and institutions that underpinned authoritarianism have either endured directly or partially into the democratic period with significant consequences for progressive governments that have taken office. Recent and ongoing attacks on the Brazilian President Dilma Rousseff and former President Luiz Inácio Lula da Silva by judges allied to the political right illustrate this clearly; so, too, does the experience of populist movements in Armenia, where a popular uprising successfully overthrew the illiberal democratic regime of Serzh Sargsyan only to find that the dominant institutions that remained were largely unchanged and staffed by supporters of the previous regime, with whom the new pro-democracy government had to work.

Thus, the end of the Cold War ushered in an era shaped by two major elite discourses whose ideas resonate in the current period of populism: the end of history and the triumph of liberal capitalist democracy; but also its dystopian counterpart, the clash of civilizations, according to which quasi-apocalyptic view the end of the Cold War ushered in a new age of global conflict between cultures rather than over economic or ideological interests.

The end of history and the post-Cold War extension and deepening of capitalism are central to understanding the rise of contemporary populist movements. As Immanuel Wallerstein has noted, the triumph of the market has posed a number of apparently irresolvable problems for political elites, who have become increasingly vulnerable to the demands of capital for profit, and the conflicting demands of the general population for higher wages, public services, and welfare. Hence the concept of the 1% versus the 99%, which emerged during the Occupy movement, was an expression of the polarizing nature of post-Cold War capitalism and the sharp increase in global inequality that has occurred. Interestingly both progressive and reactionary populist social movements share this critique of capitalism and globalization while diverging sharply on the correct response to it.

The end of the Cold War was also seen by many as the historic demise of the left, with the collapse of communism or the transformation of social democratic parties into various shades of neoliberalism. This latter trend is a marked pattern across the MWS and has seen social democratic parties retreat from their historic constituencies into a more open embrace of capitalism as they search for legitimacy among capitalists and the financial markets. Nonetheless, a number of factors recur here in explaining the rise of populist social movements: growing inequality and the increasing precarity of working lives; the growing indebtedness of the world's population, particularly the young and university graduates; and the fear that democratic politics, having become detached from the electorate, are now the preserve of unaccountable elites.

At the same time, the clash of civilizations discourse has also manifested itself in the emergence of reactionary populist social movements that are rooted in a separatist ethnic nationalism and have an essentialist orientation towards social identity. The logical consequence of this is to further embed discrimination and racism into mainstream political discourses and policies. These themes manifest themselves in specific kinds of populist social movements that can be seen across the MWS, and importantly, in major political parties and governments that have become increasingly powerful and popular in multiple countries. Many of these groups are reacting with hostility towards globalization and cosmopolitanism, which they believe will lead to the erosion of traditional social values, and transfer sovereignty from the people to technocratic elites.

The recent installation of Carlo Cottarelli as the Italian Prime Minister is a case in point; here, a former IMF official is chosen as Prime Minister of a country which had voted for a political program critical of the European Union (EU). For populist movements this is an illustration of the way in which political and economic decisions are taken without regard for the wishes of the people. For reactionary populists, it is a reflection of the cosmopolitan and liberal elite's subversion of the nation in defense of globalization; for progressive populists, it is a move that defends the EU from the people, but the EU in this case is viewed as a project to deepen and defend capitalism across members states and promote austerity measures at the expense of public services.

The appeal of ethnic nationalist populism is in part then its defense of sovereignty and the people against a number of "external' threats."[3] This defensive posture towards outsiders simultaneously generates an inclusive, positive form of identity politics for those deemed to "belong" due to their ethnic characteristics, however defined. More pointedly, in Central and Eastern Europe this kind of populism has draped itself in socialist clothing by claiming to stand up for welfare, properly paid jobs, support for the elderly, and so on. These reactionary populist movements, despite their social messages, are rooted in the preservation of traditional forms of hierarchy and social order, which are seen as being threatened by the spread of a global and cosmopolitan capitalism. This does not make these groups anti-capitalist; instead they more often represent a return to the kind of national capitalist strategy of the inter-war period: a strong state to protect the national market and segments of the population under an authoritarian social order.

There have also been very different kinds of populist movements emerging in the post-Cold War period that have embraced cosmopolitan outlooks and defended universality as the basis for a good society; among the universal values they embrace are liberty, solidarity, equality and democracy. Thus, from the Zapatista uprising in 1994 through to Occupy in 2011, progressive populism has articulated a critique of the inequalities that characterize the MWS, and they have done so in rhetorically powerful ways (e.g. the 99% vs. the 1%). However, thus far at least, these movements have not been able to build a lasting and sustained organization that could generate enduring social change. For the reactionary right-wing populist movements the goals are easier: to assume state power and use this authority to reshape social life in ways that reinforce traditional hierarchies and social divisions. For progressive social movements, the goals are more complex and therefore more difficult to attain. If the state is viewed as being a problem because of its violence, coercion, protection of privilege and inequality, is the goal to take over the state, or is it something else? For reactionary populist movements, the key to mobilization of the people is to combine tactics like stoking fear of foreigners with an appeal to national identity, wrapped in an often irrational and intolerant nationalism. By contrast, progressive populism has to appeal to reason as a basis for mobilizing people around a defense of Enlightenment ideals of equality, liberty and solidarity.

Conclusions: Principles and Pitfalls

Populism, of course, is not new; it has a lengthy lineage in the MWS. The argument made here is that the contemporary division between types of populist movements can be traced back to the Enlightenment and is a manifestation of a very old conflict between universalism and nationalism. The basis for a progressive social order cannot be built on national identity, because, ultimately, what Mestrovic distinguishes as good (civic) nationalism invariably bleeds into bad (ethnic) nationalism. To be clear, the road to the Holocaust was built by nationalist ideologies of the Anti-Enlightenment, not the Enlightenment itself. The road to the gulag, too, was built on the basis of Stalin's nationalist chauvinism and authoritarian bolshevism, not on the Enlightenment ideals of preserving individual liberty. Indeed, one of the major failings of Marxism as political practice has been precisely its willingness to sacrifice the individual on the basis of an appeal to the objective interests of the working classes. By contrast, the progressive populist movements that have emerged in this period have shown a sensitivity to multiple forms of oppression and illegitimate authority, which they continue to struggle to overturn. They have also, in many instances, shown a resistance to the Marxist legacy of vanguardism and doctrinal purity, which, over the course of the Twentieth Century left a legacy of authoritarianism that seriously undermined the case for socialism amongst the uncommitted.

[...]

Notes

1 See *United Nations Sustainable Development Goals*: https://www.un.org/sustainabledevelopment/sustainable-development-goals/.

2 Witness the revival of U.S.-backed death squads in El Salvador and Russian violence in the Ukraine. Equally the end of the Cold War has also ushered in a new era of global violence and warfare with the core being the main driver of this, sanctioning wars that stretch from Europe to Africa and the Middle East with colossal death tolls.

3 Take, for example, the UK's *Britain First* party.

Nationalism Is Patriotism Gone Wrong

Mona Charen

Mona Charen is an American journalist and political commentator. She is a senior fellow at the Ethics and Public Policy Center and has contributed to CNN, National Review, *and the* New York Times.

National Review has sparked an important debate about nationalism. As someone who has been accused throughout her life of excessive love of country (can't count the number of times I've been reproached for arguing that despite slavery, Jim Crow, and the internment of Japanese Americans, our country is eminently lovable), I feel a bit awkward rebutting anything that travels under the name "Love of Country." Nevertheless, I must join Jonah Goldberg, Ben Shapiro, and others in demurring from Rich Lowry's and Ramesh Ponnuru's defense of nationalism.

Lowry and Ponnuru are two of the writers I most admire (at a time when that group is shrinking fast). If they make an argument with which I disagree, I'm inclined to question my own judgment. So I remain open to the possibility that they are right. But it seems to me that their willingness to believe that nationalism, as opposed to patriotism, can be benign is not convincing.

Everything they assert about the naturalness of nationalism—it arises out of the same soil as love of family, community, church, etc.—is true of patriotism. It's true, as Lowry and Ponnuru note, that the Left has discredited itself over the years by its hostility to sincere patriotism.

Patriotism is enough—it needs no improving or expanding. Nationalism is something else. It's hard to think of a nationalist who does not pervert patriotism into something aggressive—either against foreign adversaries or against domestic minorities, or both. When Mexican president Lázaro Cárdenas nationalized the oil industry in 1938 (expropriating the property of hated foreigners), he was favored with a chanting crowd of 100,000 supporters in Mexico City. Gamal Abdel Nasser's nationalism also found expression in nationalization (of the Suez Canal, in that case) and also in aggressive war against Israel and Yemen. Putin's nationalism has been characterized by demonization of the United States in domestic propaganda and invasion of neighboring countries. Mussolini believed in reclaiming Italy's lost glory and invaded Abyssinia (Ethiopia) to fulfill his vision.

Our own history is not pristine. We've had our moments of belligerent nationalism. The Mexican–American War, for example, was a pure land grab. Lowry and Ponnuru cite Lincoln as an example of a benign nationalist, but he recognized corrupt nationalism in his own time. As a member of Congress, he deplored the Mexican–American War in the strongest terms, accusing President Polk of misleading the public about whose territory hostilities began on, and thundering that "the blood of this war, like the blood of Abel, is crying out to Heaven." I'm not proposing that we return California to the Mexicans (though considering their voting patterns, it's tempting), but the war that brought California (and other states) into our union was not our finest hour. It was, arguably, the hour of maximal American nationalism.

I believe that nationalism is a demagogue's patriotism. Demagogues of the Right and Left both play upon natural and even benevolent instincts for their own purposes. The Left's demagogues distort love of justice and equality into a leveling desire to scapegoat others. Bernie Sanders doesn't just appeal to people's desire for fairness, he encourages them to believe that they are the victims of the "1 percent," who are siphoning all of the nation's wealth for themselves. If you are poor, Sanders claims, it is because someone who is rich has taken your share.

Demagogues of the Right—or nationalists—argue that our troubles are the result of immigrants' taking our jobs or foreigners' stealing our factories. This is not natural love of home and hearth or reverence for America's founding ideals; it is scapegoating.

Which brings us to the proximate cause of this debate—President Trump. Far from deepening our appreciation of our history or institutions, he embodies the reasons to be wary of demagoguery in the name of country. In him we see strutting nationalism ("America first"!) but little true patriotism. He claims to pursue America's interests, yet has shockingly little respect for the nation he heads. He doesn't love the country enough to have familiarized himself with the basics of our system. In one debate, he said judges "sign bills," and in a Capitol Hill meeting with congressmen, he praised Article XII of the Constitution. What patriot can claim that we lack the moral authority to criticize Turkey's crackdown on independent journalists, or impugn this country as no better than Russia when it comes to political assassination? As Trump demonstrates, nationalism is not patriotism in a hurry—it is resentment draped in the flag.

In his concurrence with Lowry/Ponnuru, John O'Sullivan indirectly makes a similar point, defending Trump's disavowal of American exceptionalism. O'Sullivan offers that this is delicacy on Trump's part. "He doesn't want to humiliate the foreigners who will shortly be losing to America…When you intend to shoot a man, it costs nothing to be polite."

That's not my idea of patriotism.

The Distinction Is Complicated, but Patriotism and Nationalism Represent Different Things

Slavica Jakelić

Slavica Jakelić is a professor of humanities and social thought at Valparaiso University and an associate fellow at the Institute for Advanced Studies in Culture, where she directed the Secularism in the Late Modern Age *project.*

In his conversation with Religion & Its Publics Senior Fellows, E.J. Dionne argues that America needs a new patriotism. This is a patriotism grounded in ideals: it begins with the "pride in our ability to absorb newcomers…the pride in their intense desire to become Americans" and, together with empathy, it can rejuvenate American democratic culture so that the ideal of political freedom is not enacted only through conflict but also through consensus.

We also hear from Dionne that patriotism supplies an answer to politics of divisions that triumphed in Trump's election. As he writes in his book "One Nation After Trump", co-authored with Norman J. Ornstein and Thomas E. Mann, that victory successfully linked "populism, nationalism, nativism, and protectionism," thus threatening the institutions of American democracy, especially its commitment to pluralism. (In that they agree with EJ's colleague at the Brookings Institution, William Galston).

Calls for a new patriotism accurately identify two challenges: first, the need to respond to a moment in which it is the populists who most successfully articulate the notions of collective identity (defining the "we" as the hegemonic power of "the people" against, vertically, "the elite" and, horizontally, minorities) and second, the demand to put forward a constructive notion of what binds Americans to each other *while* they remain

"Pluralizing Nationalism, Or Why 'New Patriotism' Might Not Be an Answer," by Slavica Jakelić, Religion and Its Publics, June 20, 2018. Reprinted by permission.

different from each other. The constructive aspect of the task is most challenging—to shape a collectivity, respect pluralism, and, in Jason Springs's apt phrase, allow for a "healthy conflict." But to get there, is it a new patriotism or a new nationalism that is needed? I have suggested in another post why nationalism cannot be conflated with populism. Here I want to problematize another distinction, the one between patriotism and nationalism:

George Orwell, to whom Dionne refers, famously argued that patriotism is about a devotion to a place and a way of life, while nationalism is about power and blind loyalty to one's country that places it beyond good and evil. Philosophers tell us that patriotism is about the love of country, and nationalism is about love of one group of people with whom one shares ethnic or historical bonds. They also instruct us that patriotism can be shaped in accord with virtue and morality. It can be, to use Igor Primoratz's term, "ethical," asking whether policies and institutions of one's country are just, domestically and internationally. Nationalism, we are told, is always about special love for one's people. Here, loyalty precedes morality and attachments precede moral concerns.

As with any neat list of conceptual distinctions, the problem with this one is that even those who elaborate it often blur the differences between patriotism and nationalism, sometimes conflating the two notions altogether. (Dionne, for example, moves without explanation from patriotism to the "*national* culture we share and shape.") The second problem with patriotism-nationalism distinctions is how they fuse conceptual thinking with the act of political moralizing: nationalism is emptied of any ethical force while patriotism is imbued with moral content in ways that all to easily get us to claims that we are patriots while *they* are nationalists. There is yet another difficulty with neat patriotism-nationalism differentiation, this one directly related to the patriotism advocates's desire to shape a response to nativism, a response that allows both for plurality and bonds of identity. This problem emerges from the view of patriotism as individualistic, reasonable, and open to contestations, and of nationalism as collectivistic, visceral, and exclusivist.

Despite the messiness or impossibility of patriotism-nationalism distinctions—as conceptually discussed or practically enacted—I want to suggest that patriotism is always posited as an ethical ideal in terms of a capacity to reconcile one's responsibility to her community *and* the sovereignty of the individual. The concern with individualism, against all forms of collectivisms, is the background of Orwell's understanding of nationalism; individualism is also at stake in the discussions of philosophers, political theorists, and public figures mentioned here. They know that *something* is needed to bind individuals into a meaningful democratic polity but reject nationalism seeing it as collectivistic and ultimately violent.

Such concerns about nationalism are justified: nothing taught me more about nationalism's hegemonic and violent faces than the brutality of the 1990s war in my own country, Croatia. Yet, this does not change my doubts about the purported moral promise of patriotism and its superiority over nationalism, and my earlier invitation to pluralize our thinking about nationalism. Hence my questions:

Can one's love of a *place* bind an individual to others, into a meaningful democratic political community that has long been divided? Can one's pride about one's country's ideals heal divisions that result also from the historical practices her country wants to forget? Can the individualistic locus of patriotism take on the collective force of populist narratives of belonging and exclusion?

Or, could critical and historically conscious narratives of national belonging provide a framework of identity that more powerfully confront nativisms of our time? I am thinking here of narratives that arise in the protests of kneeling NFL players. Their resistance to racial injustices is not their rejection but a way to claim and redefine the American identity. But I am also thinking here of a need for more pluralistic intellectual accounts of nationalism—the ones that recognize that a history of nationalisms in any given case is plural and a story of contestations among various narratives, and the accounts of nationalism that, in remembering and probing one nation's history in *all* its facets, enable critique but also a reflexive formation of attachments.

In the 19th century, historian Ernest Renan argued that, to get a nation, you must get its history wrong. In the 21st century, we could claim, to get a nation, it is necessary to get its history right. Can a patriotism that is individualistic, empathetic, and selective in remembering accomplish this? Or, could a reflexive approach to nationalisms, past and present, shape an *ethical nationalism* that can forge another way forward and reject the populists' attempts to claim the domain of collective identity only as their own?

Passivity Distinguishes Patriotism from Nationalism

Sandipan Deb

Sandipan Deb is an Indian journalist and the editorial director at Swarajya *magazine. He previously served in editorial roles at* OPEN, *the* Financial Express, *and* Outlook *and studied at the Indian Institute of Technology Kharagpur.*

Over the last fortnight, we have seen a pitched battle in India—between "nationalists" and "liberals." After all, for most liberal elites, both in India and the West, nationalism is a dangerous, regressive and divisive impulse.

During the current Indo-Pak crisis, several liberals quoted from George Orwell's classic 1945 essay *Notes On Nationalism*, where he distinguished between patriotism and nationalism. Patriots, wrote Orwell, are devoted to a particular place and way of life, which they believe to be the world's best but have no wish to force on others. "Patriotism is of its nature defensive, both militarily and culturally. Nationalism, on the other hand, is inseparable from the desire for power. The abiding purpose of every nationalist is to secure more power and more prestige, not for himself but for the nation or other unit in which he has chosen to sink his own individuality." However, no liberal quoted from later in the essay, where Orwell also condemns pacifists ("transferred nationalists") and Anglophobists ("negative nationalists"): "Pacifist propaganda usually boils down to saying that one side is as bad as the other, but if one looks closely…, one finds that (their disapproval is) directed almost entirely against Britain and the United States. Moreover, they do not as a rule condemn violence as such, but only violence used in defence of western countries." Replace "Britain and the

"Opinion | Liberals are losing the ideological battle against nationalism," by Sandipan Deb, Live Mint, March 10, 2019. Used by permission.

United States" and "western countries" with "India" in some liberal laments in mainstream and social media, and you will get my point.

As for Anglophobia, "Within the intelligentsia, a derisive and mildly hostile attitude towards Britain is more or less compulsory.... Many people were undisguisedly pleased when Singapore fell or when the British were driven out of Greece, and there was a remarkable unwillingness to believe in good news, e.g. El Alamein, or the number of German planes shot down in the Battle of Britain. English left-wing intellectuals did not, of course, actually want the Germans or Japanese to win the war, but many of them could not help getting a certain kick out of seeing their own country humiliated."

Even sociologist-turned-politician Yogendra Yadav, who is as liberal as they come, wrote in *Theprint.in*, post-Pulwama: "Our post-Independence liberal elite feels awkward about nationalism. Like the European elite, we have started associating nationalism with negativity, jingoism and ethnic supremacists. In doing so, we have cut ourselves off from the rich and inclusivist legacy of Indian nationalism. We want to live in a modern nation-state without caring for our nationhood."

If we go by Orwell's definition, that a patriot believes that his particular place or way of life is the best, isn't that a bit woolly-headed and closed-minded? On the other hand, I know quite a few nationalists who do not believe that India is the world's best country and often complain about the problems our country suffers from. Several of them are trying to do something about it.

I believe that patriotism is a passive form of nationalism. Patriotism cannot exist without a nation, and a nation cannot survive without nationalism. It is one of the modern world's foundational principles. Nationalism gave rise to the modern state system and was a liberating force in anticolonial freedom struggles across the globe. Democracy is a result of the creation of nation-states.

One of Karl Marx's biggest mistakes was to assume that the working classes would rise above their national identities and never fight each other. Millions have died in wars since then, and the proletariat have invariably chosen nationalism over their supposed class interests.

The European Union has hardly been able to contain its members' nationalistic agendas and universal cosmopolitanism will always remain confined to John Lennon's *Imagine*.

Today, nationalism is more important than ever before as we have to balance national interests with the demands of a globalized economy and changing geopolitics. Mere patriotism will not do. Nationalistic China is attempting to build a global empire (while boxing in India). Russia has transnational ambitions. Orwell called patriotism "defensive, both militarily and culturally." India has been defensive for far too long. In an increasingly competitive world, we have to push our interests harder. We need more, not less, nationalism.

Of course, nationalism can get perverted—but let us term those outcomes more precisely as jingoism and chauvinism, not as one-label-fits-all nationalism. As Yael Tamir, former member of the Israeli Knesset, writes: "When liberals indiscriminately attack all forms of nationalism, they fuel an unnecessary ideological struggle, one that they are currently losing."

We need to develop better forms of nationalism, through every form of inclusion—social, political, financial—not through demagoguery or empty symbolism but by instilling true pride in every Indian heart. For that, we need something else too. As Swami Vivekananda said (and I paraphrase): You can't expect someone to worship God on an empty stomach. Similarly, you can't expect a household that can't afford two meals a day to be very nationalistic. Or liberal.

Progressive Patriotism Is Distinct from Nationalism

Peter Dreier and Dick Flacks

Peter Dreier is the E. P. Clapp Distinguished Professor of Politics and chair of the urban and environmental policy department at Occidental College. Dick Flacks is a research professor of sociology at the University of California, Santa Barbara.

If the news stories leading up to July 4 are any indication, media coverage of our national Independence Day celebration will focus on the competing images of Donald Trump's dictator-like display of American militarism and the efforts of an extremist lunatic to burn an American flag to protest Trumpism. Both of these endeavors are absurd distortions of patriotism and should be condemned by Americans across the political spectrum, but especially by progressives.

Trump has decided to waste taxpayer money by celebrating July 4 with a costly military parade and flyovers in Washington, D.C. before delivering a speech at the Lincoln Memorial. On Tuesday morning, Trump, a draft dodger, tweeted that "The Pentagon & our great Military Leaders are thrilled to be doing this & showing to the American people, among other things, the strongest and most advanced Military anywhere in the World." Surely Abraham Lincoln will be rolling in his grave as Trump bellows his racist, nativist and bullying bombast from the steps in front of the memorial to our 16th president.

The media have been reporting that anti-Trump protesters will be on hand to challenge the president's patriotic vision, including some who hope to fly the "Baby Trump" balloon over the parade. But, unfortunately, many news stories have focused on the plans of one lone lunatic who has pledged to burn an American flag to symbolize his disdain for the president. That lunatic is Gregory Lee "Joey" Johnson, an extremist affiliated with the Revolutionary Communist Party, a

"Progressive Patriotism for July 4," by Peter Dreier and Dick Flacks, Common Dreams, July 4, 2019. Reprinted by permission.

tiny fringe cult that couldn't be more marginal to American politics. Since Trump took office, millions of Americans have protested in the streets in opposition to his views and policies, and not one of them has burned an American flag. Giving Johnson, who represents nobody, any publicity at all is an act of journalistic malpractice.

In 1968, in a famous speech against the Vietnam war, Norman Thomas, the aging leader of the Socialist Party, proclaimed, "I come to cleanse the American flag, not burn it." That is the appropriate way for Americans to express their patriotism and protest Trump.

As both a candidate and as president, Trump has consistently confused patriotism and nationalism. According to the Merriam Webster dictionary, patriotism is a "love for or devotion to one's country." In contrast, nationalism is a "sense of national consciousness exalting one nation above all others and placing primary emphasis on promotion of its culture and interests as opposed to those of other nations or supranational groups."

Trump doesn't understand that the ways Americans express their patriotism are as diverse as our nation.

To some, patriotism means "my country—right or wrong." To others, it means loyalty to a set of principles, and thus requires dissent and criticism when those in power violate those standards. One version of patriotism suggests "Love it or leave it." The other version means "Love it and fix it."

This is a longstanding debate in American history.

Former President George W. Bush questioned the patriotism of anyone who challenged his war on terrorism. In his 2001 State of the Union address, for example, Bush claimed, "You're either with us, or with the terrorists." He introduced the Patriot Act to codify this view, giving the government new powers to suppress dissent. (The anti-war movement countered with bumper stickers illustrated with an American flag that proclaimed "Peace is Patriotic.")

In contrast, President Barack Obama said: "I have no doubt that, in the face of impossible odds, people who love their country can change it." He observed that, "Loving your country shouldn't just mean watching fireworks on the Fourth of July. Loving your country must mean accepting your responsibility to do your part to change it. If you do, your life will be richer, our country will be stronger."

Obama was echoing the words of Rev. Martin Luther King, who declared, in a speech during the Montgomery bus boycott in 1955, "the great glory of American democracy is the right to protest for right."

At a speech to the American Legion in Cincinnati during his campaign, Trump said, "We want young Americans to recite the Pledge of Allegiance." He promised the war veterans that he would work "to strengthen respect for our flag." He pledged that: "We will be united by our common culture, values and principles, becoming one American nation, one country under one constitution saluting one American flag—and always saluting it—the flag all of you helped to protect and preserve, that flag deserves respect."

Of course, many Americans believe that Trump has brought shame, not respect, on the American flag. His brand of flag-waving patriotism is rooted in xenophobia and racism. Only some kinds of people, Trump believes, deserve to be Americans.

At a campaign rally in Tampa, as his cult followers chanted "build that wall," Trump interrupted his speech to give a bear hug to an American flag on the stage behind him—apparently as a way to demonstrate his patriotism.

"We want to make sure that anyone who seeks to join our country, shares our values and has the capacity to love our people," Trump said at a rally at the Kennedy Center in 2017.

"We all salute the same great American flag," Trump said in his 2017 inauguration address—a line he has repeated in many speeches since then.

To Trump and his followers, the flag means "America First," deporting undocumented immigrants and caging their children in detention centers, restricting visitors from Muslim countries, withdrawing from the Paris climate accord and other international agreements, and engaging in bromances with dictators.

Trump and his advisors have determine that the path to re-election is for the president to label one who disagrees with him, including every Democratic candidate, as an unpatriotic socialist.

What would Trump think about Francis Bellamy, the Christian socialist who wrote the Pledge of Allegiance, or Katherine Lee Bates, the poet who penned America the Beautiful, who was not only a socialist but also a lesbian?

Progressives understand that people can disagree with their government and still love their country and its ideals. The flag, as a symbol of the nation, is not owned by the administration in power, but by the people. We battle over what it means, but all Americans—across the political spectrum—have an equal right to claim the flag as their own.

Indeed, throughout our history, many American radicals and progressive reformers have proudly asserted their patriotism. To them, America stood for basic democratic values—economic and social equality, mass participation in politics, free speech and civil liberties, elimination of the second-class citizenship of women and racial minorities, a welcome mat for the world's oppressed people. The reality of corporate power, right-wing xenophobia, and social injustice only fueled progressives' allegiance to these principles and the struggle to achieve them.

Bellamy, a Baptist minister who lived from 1855 to 1931, wrote the Pledge of Allegiance in 1892 to express his outrage at the nation's widening economic divide. He had been ousted from his Boston church for his sermons depicting Jesus as a socialist, and for his work among the poor in the Boston slums.

It was the Gilded Age, an era marked by major political, economic, and social conflicts. Progressive reformers were outraged by the widening gap between rich and poor, and the behavior of corporate robber barons who were exploiting workers, gouging consumers, and corrupting politics with their money. Workers were organizing unions. Farmers were joining forces in the so-called Populist movement to rein in the power of banks, railroads and utility companies. Reformers fought for child labor laws, against slum housing and in favor of women's suffrage. Socialists and other leftist radicals were gaining new converts.

In foreign affairs, Americans were battling over the nation's role in the world. America was beginning to act like an imperial power, justifying its expansion with a combination of white supremacy, manifest destiny and the argument that it was spreading democracy. At the time, nativist groups across the country were pushing for restrictions on immigrants—Catholics, Jews, and Asians—who were cast as polluting Protestant America. In the South, the outcome of the Civil War still inflamed regional passions. Many Southerners, including Civil War veterans, swore allegiance not to the American but to the Confederate flag.

Bellamy, a cousin of Edward Bellamy, author of two bestselling radical books, Looking Backward and Equality, believed that unbridled capitalism, materialism, and individualism betrayed America's promise. He hoped that the Pledge of Allegiance would promote a different moral vision to counter the rampant greed he argued was undermining the nation.

When composing the Pledge, Bellamy had initially intended to use the phrase "liberty, fraternity, and equality," but concluded that the radical rhetoric of the French Revolution wouldn't sit well with many Americans. So he coined the phrase, "one nation, indivisible, with liberty and justice for all," as a means to express his more egalitarian vision of America, and a secular patriotism aimed at helping unite a divided nation.

Bellamy wrote the Pledge of Allegiance for Youth's Companion, a magazine for young people published in Boston with a circulation of about 500,000. A few years earlier, the magazine had sponsored a largely successful campaign to sell American flags to public schools. In 1891, the magazine hired Bellamy to organize a public relations campaign to celebrate the 400th anniversary of Christopher Columbus's discovery of America by promoting use of the flag in public schools.

Bellamy gained the support of the National Education Association, along with President Benjamin Harrison and Congress, for a national ritual observance in the schools, and he wrote the Pledge of Allegiance as part of the program's flag salute ceremony.

Bellamy thought such an event would be a powerful expression on behalf of free public education. Moreover, he wanted all the schoolchildren of America to recite the pledge at the same moment. He hoped the pledge would promote a moral vision to counter the individualism embodied in capitalism and expressed in the climate of the Gilded Age.

In 1923, over the objections of the aging Bellamy, the National Flag Conference, led by the American Legion and the Daughters of the American Revolution, changed the opening, "I pledge allegiance to my flag," to "I pledge allegiance to the flag of the United States of America." Ostensibly, it was revised to make sure that immigrant children—who might have thought that "my flag" referred to their native countries—knew that they were pledging allegiance to the American flag.

In 1954, at the height of the Cold War, when many political leaders believed that the nation was threatened by godless communism—the Knights of Columbus led a successful campaign to lobby Congress to add the words "under God."

A year after Bellamy composed the Pledge, the same social conditions and political sympathies inspired Bates to write the poem America the Beautiful, which was later set to music written by Samuel Ward, the organist at Grace Episcopal Church in Newark, New Jersey. (The Mormon Tabernacle Choir sang their song at Trump's inauguration).

Like Bellamy, Bates was a Christian socialist. A well-respected poet and professor of English at Wellesley College, Bates (1859-1929) was also a lesbian who lived with and was devoted to her colleague Katharine Coman, an economics professor. They were both part of progressive circles in the Boston area that supported labor unions, advocated for immigrants, and fought for women's suffrage. She was an ardent foe of American imperialism.

America the Beautiful was initially published in 1895 to commemorate the Fourth of July. The poem is usually heard as an unalloyed paean to American virtue. But a close reading of her words makes it clear that she had something more in mind. She wrote:

> America! America!
> God shed His grace on thee
> Till selfish gain no longer stain,
> The banner of the free!

Bates hoped that a progressive movement, inspired by both religious and secular beliefs, could overcome the Gilded Age's greed.

Most Americans are unaware that much of our patriotic culture—including many of the leading symbols and songs—was created by people with decidedly progressive sympathies.

Consider the lines inscribed on the Statue of Liberty: "Give me your tired, your poor/Your huddled masses yearning to breathe free." Emma Lazarus was a poet of considerable reputation in her day, who was a strong supporter of Henry George and his "socialistic" single-tax program, and a friend of William Morris, a leading British socialist. Her welcome to the "wretched refuse" of the earth, written in 1883, was an effort to project an inclusive and egalitarian definition of the American Dream—a view clearly at odds with Trump's narrow understanding of American history and values.

In the Depression years and during World War II, the fusion of populist, egalitarian and anti-racist values with patriotic expression reached full flower.

Langston Hughes' poem, Let America Be America Again, written in 1936, contrasted the nation's promise with its mistreatment of his fellow African-Americans, the poor, Native Americans, workers, farmers and immigrants:

> O, let my land be a land where Liberty
> Is crowned with no false patriotic wreath
> But opportunity is real, and life is free
> Equality is in the air we breathe.

In 1939, composer Earl Robinson teamed with lyricist John La Touche to write Ballad for Americans, which was performed on the CBS radio network by Paul Robeson, accompanied by chorus and orchestra.

This 11-minute cantata provided a musical review of American history, depicted as a struggle between the "nobody who's everybody" and an elite that fails to understand the real, democratic essence of America.

Robeson, at the time one of the best-known performers on the world stage, became, through this work, a voice of America.

Broadcasts and recordings of Ballad for Americans (by Bing Crosby as well as Robeson) were immensely popular. In the summer of 1940, it was performed at the national conventions of both the Republican and Communist parties. The work soon became a staple in school choral performances, but it was literally ripped out of many public school songbooks after Robinson and Robeson were identified with the radical left and blacklisted during the McCarthy period. Since then, however, Ballad for Americans has been periodically revived, notably during the bicentennial celebration in 1976, when a number of pop and country singers performed it in concerts and on TV.

Aaron Copland's Fanfare for the Common Man and A Lincoln Portrait, both written in 1942, are now patriotic musical standards, regularly performed at major civic events. Few Americans know that Copland was a member of a radical composers' group.

Many Americans consider Woody Guthrie's song This Land Is Your Land, penned in 1940, to be our unofficial national anthem. Guthrie, a radical, was inspired to write the song as an answer to Irving Berlin's popular God Bless America, which he thought failed to recognize that it was the "people" to whom America belonged.

The words to This Land Is Your Land reflect Guthrie's belief that patriotism and support for the underdog were interconnected. In this song, Guthrie celebrated America's natural beauty and bounty, but criticized the country for its failure to share its riches. This is reflected in the song's last and least-known verse, which Pete Seeger and Bruce Springsteen included when they performed the song in January 2009 at a pre-inaugural concert in front of the Lincoln Memorial, with President-elect Obama in the audience:

> One bright sunny morning;
> In the shadow of the steeple;
> By the relief office;

> I saw my people.
> As they stood hungry;
> I stood there wondering;
> If this land was made for you and me.

During the 1960s, American progressives continued to seek ways to fuse their love of country with their opposition to the government's policies. The March on Washington in 1963 gathered at the Lincoln Memorial, where Martin Luther King Jr. famously quoted the words to My Country 'Tis of Thee, repeating the phrase "Let freedom ring" 11 times.

Phil Ochs, then part of a new generation of politically conscious singer-songwriters who emerged during the 1960s, wrote an anthem in the Guthrie vein, The Power and the Glory, that coupled love of country with a strong plea for justice and equality. The words to the chorus echo the sentiments of the anti-Vietnam War movement:

> Here is a land full of power and glory;
> Beauty that words cannot recall;
> Oh her power shall rest on the strength of her freedom;
> Her glory shall rest on us all.

One of its stanzas updated Guthrie's combination of outrage and patriotism:

> Yet she's only as rich as the poorest of her poor;
> Only as free as the padlocked prison door;
> Only as strong as our love for this land;
> Only as tall as we stand.

This song later became part of the repertoire of the U.S. Army band.

In recent decades, Bruce Springsteen has most closely followed in the Guthrie tradition. From Born in the USA, to his songs about Tom Joad (the militant protagonist in John Steinbeck's The Grapes of Wrath), to his anthem about the 9/11 tragedy (Empty Sky), to his album Wrecking Ball (including its opening song, We Take Care of Our Own), Springsteen has championed the downtrodden while challenging America to live up to its ideals.

Steve Van Zandt is best known as the guitarist with Springsteen's E Street Band and for his role as Silvio Dante, Tony Soprano's sidekick on the TV show, The Sopranos. But his most enduring legacy should be his love song about America, I Am a Patriot, including these lyrics:

> I am a patriot, and I love my country;
> Because my country is all I know.
> Wanna be with my family;
> People who understand me;
> I got no place else to go.
> And I ain't no communist,
> And I ain't no socialist,
> And I ain't no capitalist,
> And I ain't no imperialist,
> And I ain't no Democrat,
> Sure ain't no Republican either,
> I only know one party,
> And that is freedom.

Since the American Revolution, each generation of progressives has expressed an American patriotism rooted in democratic values that challenged jingoism and "my country—right or wrong" thinking. They rejected blind nationalism, militaristic drum beating, and sheep-like conformism.

Throughout the United States' history, they have viewed their movements—abolition of slavery, farmers' populism, women's suffrage, workers' rights, civil rights, environmentalism, gay rights, and others—as profoundly patriotic. They believed that America's core claims—fairness, equality, freedom, justice—were their own.

America now confronts a new version of the Gilded Age, brought upon by Wall Street greed and corporate malfeasance. The gap between rich and poor is still widening. Although the economy has improved in recent years, Americans are feeling more economically insecure than at any time since the Depression. They are upset by the unbridled selfishness and political influence-peddling demonstrated by banks, oil companies, drug companies, insurance companies, and other large corporations. They are angry at the growing power of American-based global firms who show no loyalty to their country, outsource jobs to low-wage countries, avoid paying taxes, and pollute the environment.

With Trump in the White House, we are, once again, battling over immigration and who belongs in America. With Trump's approval, right-wing groups and talk-show pundits, calling themselves patriots, have unleashed a new wave of hate and bigotry.

Trump claims he wants to "make America great again" and "bring jobs home." But those sentiments conflict with Trump's own business practices. The entire Donald J. Trump Collection of clothing—including men's dress shirts, suits, ties and accessories—was made in factories overseas, mostly in China, Bangladesh, and Central America, to take advantage of cheap labor.

Trump followed in the tradition of Sam Walton, the founder of Walmart, America's largest corporation, who promoted the motto "Buy American." But today the retail giant, now owned by his heirs, imports most of its merchandise from Asia, much of it made under inhumane sweatshop conditions.

Trump's nativism, xenophobia, racism, selfishness, materialism, and faux patriotism would have appalled Francis Bellamy. Trump may want to require American schoolchildren to recite the Pledge of Allegiance, but his vision of America is a far cry from Bellamy's—or any progressive who fights to push the country to live up to its ideals.

Over the past few years, efforts like Occupy Wall Street, Black Lives Matter, the Dreamers immigrant-rights movement, the battles against the Keystone pipeline and for marriage equality, the MeToo movement, and the Fight for $15 (minimum wage) campaign have generated a new wave of activism, but nothing has inspired more protest and resistance than Trump.

This movement, which embodies the Pledge of Allegiance's idea of "liberty and justice for all," reflects America's tradition of progressive patriotism. It recognizes that conservatives don't have a monopoly on Old Glory.

Happy July 4th.

From the Perspective of Racial Discrimination, There Is Little Difference Between Nationalism and Nativism

Jelani Cobb and Nilagia McCoy

Jelani Cobb is the Ira A. Lippman Professor of Journalism at Columbia University. From 2012-16, he served as Director of the Institute for African American Studies at the University of Connecticut at Storrs. Nilagia McCoy is Communications Manager at the Center for Innovation in Social Work and Health at Boston University.

Jelani Cobb, A.M. Rosenthal Writer-in-Residence at the Shorenstein Center and staff writer for The New Yorker, discussed the influence of history on current events, changing demographics in the U.S., the media's coverage of racial issues, and more during a talk at the Center. Below are some highlights from his conversation with Shorenstein Center Director Nicco Mele, with the full audio to be posted soon.

Understanding Today's Populism Through the Lens of the Past

"A lot of times, I think we use the word populism in an attempt to be euphemistic, because we were seeing racism, xenophobia, nativism, this really delusional, conspiratorial thinking—and so the polite way of expressing that was just to say, 'oh this is populism'—until we actually get into what the history of populism has looked like in this country. A very wide swath of it has been racist, nativist, xenophobic, and susceptible to really bizarre, conspiratorial analyses of the world...I was looking at the populist movements that arose in the late 19th century in the South and the ways in which they had a really striking degree of interracial cooperation and suspicion of economic forces in a way that would be familiar to people on the liberal, left side of the political equation now. And then, just around the very end of the 19th century and the beginning of the 20th century, those movements collapsed and what emerged was a kind of uniform negrophobia and a very aggressive white nationalist version of populism that connects to much of what we've seen now."

Queens, New York As a Bellwether of Demographic Change

"I don't think we can overstate the importance of Trump being from Queens in the narrative that we've seen play out. [Queens] is statistically the most diverse county in the United States…this is all a product of the 1965 Immigration Act. Queens was one of the first places that witnessed the transformation that would become a fact of American immigration over the ensuing years and decades. But prior to that, Queens had been the second whitest borough in New York City. The Queens that I grew up in was enormously diverse. The Queens that Trump grew up in was overwhelmingly white and then became enormously diverse. So the language of nativism, the language of fear, of xenophobia…that is all part of the narrative that we're looking at in recent American politics. For Trump's generation [of] white Queens residents, many of them never got over seeing the rapid diversification of the county, the way that many people are now alarmed about the diversification of the country."

Political Representation and Diversity

"Roof did what he did—murdering nine people in the sanctuary of their church—for propaganda purposes. He was trying to encourage white people to recognize that they were being taken advantage of, and that they were being put in a subordinate position…the fact that there was not a clear delineation of white over black as there had been in South Carolina's history previously was what was disturbing to him, and he wanted the reassertion of that."

"When I saw Charlottesville happen, and the mass mobilization of people under this banner—armies of whiteness that we've seen before in American history—it was like a response. Roof was a call and what happened [in Charlottesville] was a response. Much of what we saw electorally was a response. I went to some of those Trump rallies. The reaction that people had—this is not about economic anxiety. This is about something else. I'm not implying a causal relationship...Roof said that he was killing these people because he wanted to protect white women from black rapists. Donald Trump notably and outrageously said that he was running in part because of all of the Mexican rapists in the country. I don't think Trump saying that caused Roof to do what he did; Roof had been scouting out the church before that. But they were responding to the same, particular historical dynamic."

The Media's Reluctance to Call Out Racism

"There should be a bar, because what we have now is that it's impossible for you to do anything that actually qualifies as being racist. It might be 'controversial' or 'racially charged'—what does that mean? That doesn't mean anything. We tend to, I think for commercial reasons, fall back on this comfortable language that, really, no decent writing teacher would allow in their class. Even things like 'race relations'—what are those? We have a relative presence or absence of racism. I don't know what 'race relations' are, unless it's a convenient way of avoiding this question of the political potency of racism in any particular point in time."

"On the one hand you have seen, I think, a much more overt stance in terms of willingness to call a spade a spade. On the other hand, The New York Times also published the Nazi next door piece, which was obscene in its evenhandedness. We don't see that much of it now, but there was a six-month period after the election where there seemed to be a directive from all the editorial offices in the country to redeem the Trump voter, to prove that they weren't racist, even though analyses of data have pointed out that Trump's xenophobia and nativism were not exceptions, they were things that appealed to people…I think generally speaking, there's still not a willingness to confront that."

On Defending Democracy

"The reason why I'm less pessimistic than I may sound at the outset is that I am also cognizant of people's capacities to defend the democratic ideal of human rights, or the ideal of human dignity, against systems that are set up for the opposite effect. I still believe in human courage and the decency of human beings, even in the context of the horrible political moment…I think we've seen a lot of that."

Anti-Globalization Is the Key to Understanding Contemporary Nationalism and Nativism

Manuela Achilles, Kyrill Kunakhovich, and Nicole Shea

Manuela Achilles is a professor of German and history and director of the European Studies Program at the University of Virginia. Kyrill Kunakhovich is a professor of history at the University of Virginia. Nicole Shea is the director of the Council for European Studies and the Executive Editor of EuropeNow.

On the evening of August 11, 2017, a large group of white supremacists, alt-right activists, and neo-Nazis—mostly men, but also a few women—staged a torchlight parade through the grounds of the University of Virginia. Chanting, "You will not replace us" and "Jews will not replace us," they marched to a statue of the university's founder, Thomas Jefferson, where they attacked a small group of students, faculty, and staff. The next morning, a much larger crowd—as many as 500 people—gathered a mile away, in downtown Charlottesville, around a statue of Confederate general Robert E. Lee. Participants wielded shields, battle flags, and semi-automatic weapons; they harassed and assaulted local residents who had lined the streets in protest until the police broke up the rally. A small group then adjourned to a nearby park, where they listened to speeches by rally organizers. Meanwhile, a rally participant rammed his car into a downtown crosswalk, killing a young woman, Heather Heyer, and injuring nineteen others.

To observers and participants alike, this American tragedy resonated with echoes of Europe. Most striking were the Nazi symbols, which seemed like relics from another age: swastikas, the Black Sun, cries of "blood and soil." But there were also more contemporary links.

"Nationalism, Nativism, and the Revolt Against Globalization," by Manuela Achilles, Kyrill Kunakhovich, and Nicole Shea, EuropeNow, February 1, 2018. This article first appeared in the journal EuropeNow. Reprinted by permission.

One participant carried a shield with the slogan "nog är nog," Swedish for "enough is enough," which is used by Sweden's anti-immigration activists. The chant "You will not replace us" originated with Identity Evropa, a US-based group that calls itself a "generation of awakened Europeans."[1] It is an offshoot of the Identitarian movement that began in France and has close ties to Germany's anti-Islamic front, PEGIDA. The rally's main organizer, Richard Spencer, runs a so-called think tank "dedicated to the heritage, identity and future of European people."[2] Another speaker, Matthew Heimbach, models himself on the Romanian fascist Corneliu Codreanu and calls Russia the "leader of the free world."[3]

Such contacts suggest that the Charlottesville rally was part of a broader movement—and indeed Europe saw many similar rallies in 2017. Perhaps the biggest took place in Warsaw in November, when some 60,000 people marched to chants of "pure blood" and "white Europe."[4] Anti-immigrant demonstrations are on the rise across the continent, and so, too, are anti-immigrant assaults. Over 3,500 (nearly 10 a day) were recorded in Germany in 2016 alone,[5] including 595 beatings and 116 arson attacks.[6] Such violence in the streets has only strengthened far-right parties at the ballot box. In the past year, the Alternative for Germany and the Austrian People's Party placed third in their countries' parliamentary elections, while the Dutch Party for Freedom finished second. By political scientist Matt Golder's account, "far right parties have participated in coalition governments in Austria, Croatia, Estonia, Finland, Italy, Latvia, the Netherlands, Poland, Serbia, Slovakia, and Switzerland, and they have supported minority governments in Bulgaria, Denmark, the Netherlands, and Norway."[7]

This special issue examines the resurgence of far-right groups, considering how recent events in Charlottesville can illuminate radical movements in Europe. It focuses on three key elements: nationalism, nativism, and the revolt against globalization. Nationalism was the word most associated with the Charlottesville rally, whose participants often called themselves "white nationalists." By this, they meant that a racialized national identity should be the condition for political belonging. For Spencer, the dream is a racial "ethno-state" to be achieved through what he calls "peaceful ethnic cleansing."[8]

The notion that the political and the national unit should be congruent is broadly in line with Ernest Gellner's famous definition of nationalism as "primarily a political principle, which holds that the political and the national unit should be congruent."[9] However, the commitment to a perfect synthesis of state and nation can take many forms. It can mean banning Muslim headscarves, as French courts did in 2010, on the grounds that they run counter to republican national values such as *laïcité*, gender equality, and democracy. It can mean banning political opponents, whom leaders from Vladimir Putin to Jarosław Kaczyński routinely call "national traitors." And it is also this commitment that drives Europe's many separatist movements, which promise to align state with nation. The trouble, of course, is that those are two incommensurable units: one legal and the other "imagined," "constructed," or "voluntaristic."[10] Making them congruent, as Gellner pointed out, is likely to generate intense passions.

"Nativism," the second term guiding our inquiry, originated in the 1840s in reference to US Know Nothing party—formally called the Native American Party. While it has not been widely applied to Europe, it highlights important parallels between far-right movements on both sides of the Atlantic. Most prominently, they share an intense hostility to immigrants, especially those of a different race or religion. Anti-immigrant sentiment, Elisabeth Ivarsflaten has found, is the thread that links the vast array of Europe's right-wing populists; it is the only grievance that has been "consistently mobilized by all successful populist right parties."[11] But what separates nativism from mere xenophobia is its eugenic obsession with blood, birth, and health. For Spencer, "'immigration' is a proxy for race": it produces a "miscegenated" nation and destroys whites' "biological and cultural continuity."[12] Such language has long been a fixture of Europe's far-right groups, which habitually describe immigrants as "parasites" and "cancers." Drawing from a deep well of anti-Semitism, they also portray ethnic minorities as sexual predators—a view aptly summed up by the portmanteau "rapefugees," often seen on PEGIDA banners. Here the body politic is clearly female, and its vital function—reproduction—threatened by migration of any kind.

Accordingly, one of the far-right's greatest bugaboos is the idea of globalization. The grievances are partly economic, fueled by fears of lost jobs and profiteering elites. The rhetoric of two worlds, a "France of winners" and a "France of losers," was a fixture of the 2017 presidential elections. But the concerns with globalization run deeper. For Richard Spencer, it impinges on the natural order of things, mixing together what is properly kept apart. "Identitarianism acknowledges the incommensurable nature of different peoples and cultures," he writes, "and thus looks forward to a world of true diversity and multiculturalism."[13] Europe's far-right groups view globalization as an assault on national sovereignty and identity. Marine Le Pen, in her first campaign speech, equated globalization with "Islamic fundamentalism," since "both are working to make our nation disappear."[14] Such critiques engender a politics of outrage, fueled by a sense of being under siege. That is why Charlottesville's rally centered on a statue of Lee, which the city council had recently voted to remove. Global forces like political correctness, organizers claimed, had conspired to threaten local culture—identified, in their minds, with the "lost cause" of the Confederacy.[15] The same logic drives widespread criticism of Brussels and the European Union, distant actors that are easily portrayed as meddling. It can also take overtly anti-Semitic forms: "the Goyim know," read a placard in Charlottesville, evoking the old trope of a worldwide Jewish conspiracy. The revolt against globalization frames far-right groups as underdogs, bravely fighting more powerful forces. By making the strong feel defensive, it often serves as an incitement to violence.

It is a well-known paradox that nationalism is transnational: all nations claim to be unique, but in strikingly similar ways. The same seems to be true of far-right groups, as the Charlottesville rally suggests. Such groups now share tactics, symbols, and beliefs, honed in the echo chambers of the internet, or, increasingly, through in-person meetings. In December, nine of Europe's far-right parties met in Prague to discuss joint strategy in—and against—the European Parliament. Several larger congresses have convened in Russia, which bills itself as the leader of the World National Conservative Movement. But if the global far-right is growing interconnected, so, too, are its opponents. In the days after Heather Heyer's death, "vigils for Charlottesville" took place in many European cities, from Galway to Paris to Athens. Heyer's name has also been coopted for various local causes—such as a women's protest against another far-right march in Warsaw.

Charlottesville, Virginia, has unexpectedly become a reference point in European politics, a fitting launching pad for the diverse research, interviews and art presented here to investigate nationalism, nativism, and the revolt against globalization in Europe—and beyond. Charlottesville also invites a rethinking of curricular development and pedagogical approaches as an attempted response. The *Campus* pieces draw from journalism, student and faculty testimonials as well as campus collaborations, encouraging true interdisciplinary and transatlantic dialogues as part of some pressing global issues.

Jan Willem Duyvendak and Josip Kesic's "The Rise of Nativism" considers the radical right-wing desire in the Netherlands to "preserve" the "Dutch character" as just one example of a much broader trend for monocultural purity across Europe. The paper argues that, to fully understand the various degrees and subtypes of nativist discourses, which claim to protect Europe as an entity of culture and tradition, right-wing parties must be examined through the lens of nativism with nationalism as an ideological background.

Ambassador John Shattuck, former President of Central European University, addresses the transatlantic threats to liberal democracy and global civil society, which have been exacerbated by economic, cultural, and security anxieties that liberal democracies have failed to address. Populist governments, on the other hand, capitalize on this deficiency, as the example of Hungary, where Orban has manipulated the political and even academic landscape, clearly reveals.

Once right-wing party promises are not fulfilled, many liberal voters hope, voters will see right through them and liberal democracy will be reestablished. However, the article "Poland, a 'Normal' European Country" by Agnieszka Pasieka focuses on "scorn" and "shame" to explain a long-time nationalistic orientation in a strongly polarized Polish public sphere, examining how the debate about social policies is framed and why Polish people have grown tired of "pleasing" Europe.

The events in Catalonia in the fall, spurred by political and especially harsh economic conditions during the last decade, challenge the very unity of Spain and its capacity to include diverse, cultural identities. Juan Andrés García Martín's article "The European Union, Spain and the Catalan Question: An Affair Beyond the Spanish Border?" examines the rise of Catalan nationalism, its desire for international recognition and the EU's corresponding position.

The article "Between Nativism and Indigeneity in the Kabyle Diaspora of France" by Jonathan Harris, argues that the leaders of the Kabyle diaspora, the Provisional Government of Kabylia (GPK), have assumed an ambivalent position to draw some advantages from French nativist-populist discourse, consequently, adopting a nativist populism of their own; at the same time, though, the GPK is opposed to the anti-immigration and racist elements which threaten it.

"Make America Great Again" to President Trump means the protection of his country's economic interests against multilateral "bad trade deals," calling for more national sovereignty. Peter Debaere's "Globalization Under Fire," argues that globalization per se is not the problem, but rather those who have disproportionately benefited from its gains and demonstrate an unwillingness to share. The article also argues that globalization, despite its bad press, has its benefits and that domestic protectionism is not the answer.

In populist rhetoric, migrants emerge as perceived threats to the economic and welfare systems and to culture and tradition by, for instance, "Islamizing" their new European home countries. In the curated show "Home and (Be)Longing," artist Do-Ho-Suh's translucent fabrics and mathematical processes create works built around the idea of home; however, his collapsible fabrics interrogate the connotations of "home" and "belonging." Korean-born artist Insoon Ha's work deals with the rhetoric of rape, disturbance and aggression that so often marks today's political agenda, revealing that we are far removed from equality, particularly when it comes to gender.

References

1. https://www.splcenter.org/hatewatch/2017/09/26/identity-evropa-and-arktos-media-%E2%80%94-likely-bedfellows

2. https://www.salon.com/2013/10/29/white_separatists_are_afraid_of_the_future/

3. http://www.businessinsider.com/russia-connections-to-the-alt-right-2016-11

4. https://www.washingtonpost.com/news/worldviews/wp/2017/11/12/pray-for-an-islamic-holocaust-tens-of-thousands-from-europes-far-right-march-in-poland/?utm_term=.9d0a25738a1f

5. http://www.bbc.com/news/world-europe-39096833

   http://www.dw.com/en/more-than-3500-attacks-on-refugees-in-germany-in-2016-report/a-37719365

6. https://www.proasyl.de/news/gewalt-gegen-fluechtlinge-2017-von-entwarnung-kann-keine-rede-sein/

7. Matt Golder, "Far Right Parties in Europe." The Annual Review of Political Science 19 (2016), 477-97, here 477.

8. https://www.nytimes.com/2016/11/22/world/americas/white-nationalism-explained.html

9. Ernest Gellner, Nations and Nationalism (Oxford: Blackwell, 1983), 1.

10. Benedict Anderson, Imagined Communities: Reflections on the Origins and Spread of Nationalism (London: Verso, 1983); Gellner, Nations and Nationalism, 7.

11. Elisabeth Ivarsflaten, "What Unites Right-Wing Populists in Western Europe? Re-Examining Grievance Mobilization Models in Seven Successful Cases." Comparative Political Studies 41: 1 (January 2008), 3-23, here 17.

12. https://www.splcenter.org/fighting-hate/extremist-files/individual/richard-bertrand-spencer-0

13. https://www.splcenter.org/hatewatch/2015/10/12/american-racists-work-spread-%E2%80%98identitarian%E2%80%99-ideology

14. https://www.politico.eu/article/marine-le-pen-globalization-campaign-launch-french-politics-news-lyon-islam/

15. See, e.g., Gary Gallagher and Alan T. Nolan (eds.), The Myth of the Lost Cause and Civil War History (Bloomington: Indiana University Press, 2000).

Patriotism Is Fundamentally Intertwined with Nationalism in American History

John Fonte

John Fonte is a senior fellow and director of the Center for American Common Culture at the Hudson Institute. His writing on citizenship, patriotism, and liberal democracy has appeared in Foreign Affairs, National Review, *and the* Chronicle of Higher Education.

Let us begin by playing "argument from authority," conservative style. The anti-nationalist conservatives contributing to the patriotism–nationalism debate in *National Review* have cited William F. Buckley as having said something to the effect that "I'm as patriotic as anyone from sea to shining sea, but there's not a molecule of nationalism in me." This is a paraphrase. We don't know his exact words, we don't know the context, and, therefore, we don't really know what he meant.

Now, let us go back several decades and examine the exact words and relevant context of several other prominent American conservatives who did not draw a sharp distinction between patriotism and nationalism. Then we will compare their arguments with the recent National Review essays by the proponents of an "enlightened nationalism," Rich Lowry, Ramesh Ponnuru, and John O'Sullivan, and find them complementary, but with different emphases. Finally, I will argue the patriotism and nationalism are, for good or ill, inseparable.

Frank Meyer, whose name was on the masthead of the first issue of *National Review*, is famous as a libertarian-leaning thinker who developed the conservative synthesis of "fusionism," uniting traditionalists and classical liberals. Meyer posited that an emphasis on both individual freedom and an organic moral order were philosophically and politically consistent. He wrote that this "fusionism" could (and should) form the core of conservative theory and practice. Significantly, Frank Meyer, in his article "The Booby-Trap of Internationalism" (1954), noted several times that it was regrettable that the term "nationalist," along with "patriot," had for many "become terms of reproach."

Decades later and far across the conservative political spectrum from the libertarian Meyer, two of the major godfathers of neo-conservatism, Irving Kristol and Norman Podhoretz, explicitly embraced the term "nationalism" as a positive good. In the introduction to his book *Reflections of a Neoconservative* (1983), Kristol declared, "Neoconservatism is not merely patriotic — that goes without saying—but also nationalist. Patriotism springs from love of the nation's past; nationalism arises out of hope for the nation's future, distinctive greatness. Nationalism in our time is probably the most powerful of political emotions." A decade later, in another book on neoconservatism, Kristol (as cited by Lowry and Ponnuru in their recent essay "For Love of Country") wrote, "The three pillars of modern conservatism are religion, nationalism, and economic growth."

Writing in *Commentary* a few weeks before the inauguration of Ronald Reagan in January 1981, editor Norman Podhoretz heralded a "new nationalist spirit" that had been building in America during the final Carter years. It ultimately led to Reagan's victory. Podhoretz opined, "We know from the survey data that the political mood had been shifting for some years in a consistent direction away from the self-doubts and self-hatreds . . . of the immediate post-Vietnam period and toward what some of us have called a new nationalism."

Assessing Reagan's presidency two and a half years later (July 1983), Podhoretz trumpeted a "new consensus" against totalitarian Communism. This slowly building consensus made Reagan's election possible. "We can," Podhoretz notes, "point to a palpable intensification of nationalist sentiment in the country beginning with the surprising outburst of patriotism that accompanied the bicentennial celebrations of 1976 and culminating in the pro-American demonstrations provoked by the humiliating seizure of the hostages in Iran three years later." Notice how

Podhoretz seamlessly blends patriotism and nationalism in both his overarching rhetoric (nationalist sentiment with an outburst of patriotism) and in substantive examples (bicentennial pride followed by righteous anger at the Iranian mullahs).

The context of the Kristol-Podhoretz embrace of nationalism was the emergence of a "new majority" who were upset with American weakness during the last years of the Carter administration. In short, Americans were getting tired of losing. As Podhoretz explained on January 1, 1981, "the 1980 election signified the emergence of a 'new majority' that had coalesced around Reagan's promise to work toward the restoration of American power." In 1983 Kristol wrote: "The election of 1980, for the first time, provided signs that a new Republican party might be emerging. Reagan was anything but a typical Republican candidate, and never earned the favor of the Republican establishment. . . . He came 'out of the West,' riding a horse, not a golf cart, speaking in the kind of nationalist-populist tonalities not heard since Teddy Roosevelt, appealing to large sections of the working class."

Rich Lowry and Ramesh Ponnuru argue that "nationalist sentiments are natural and can't be beaten out of people if you try" and that it "would be a strange . . . conservatism that lacked any foundation in them." In 2000, Norman Podhoretz declared that both patriotism (which he defines as "love of" one's country) and nationalism (which he defines as "pride in" one's country) is a "common feeling among peoples everywhere," and so "celebrating or condemning patriotism, and even nationalism, is rather like praising or deploring human nature itself."

Most of the participants in NR's patriotism-nationalism debate have acknowledged the significance of both the ideological and the cultural foundations of the American regime. On the creed-culture nexus, Charles Kesler has astutely observed that the American creed, although the "keystone of American national identity, . . . requires a culture to sustain it." Put otherwise, patriotic ideals require nationalist sentiments.

In a follow-up essay, Ponnuru argues that the anti-nationalist stance of "patriotism good, nationalism bad," in which positive ideals (patriotism) are pitted against various forms of (mostly ethnic) nationalism, "allows no room for a love of country that is based on both a nation's ideals and its culture." Further, it disparages any political program that emphasizes national sovereignty (over, for example, globalism) and national cohesion (over, for example, identity politics).

In contradistinction to anti-nationalism, John O'Sullivan and I have argued that American democratic nationalism can be seen "as the glue that binds economic, social, and other conservatives together, just as in the old days anti-Communism provided such as bond." We agree with Israeli philosopher Yoram Hazony, who declared that "conservatives have been nationalists since the days Disraeli wrote novels."

What about Mussolini, Putin, and Erdogan? What about politicians and theorists who exalt their country by denigrating foreigners, and what about those who glory in aggression and war? Well, we have perfectly good words for these nasty impulses, chauvinism for the former and *jingoism* for the latter. Let's use these more-precise terms rather than, painting with a broad brush, simply calling what one does not like "nationalism."

What about Adolf Hitler? John Lukacs noted that Hitler wrote in *Mein Kampf* that he was a "nationalist not a patriot." In truth, Hitler was neither a nationalist nor a patriot. In the final days of the Third Reich, he told a horrified Albert Speer, his closest confidant at the end, that the German people had proven unworthy and deserved to perish:

> It is not necessary to worry about what the German people will need for elemental survival. On the contrary, it is best for us to destroy even those things. For the nation has proven to be the weaker, and the future belongs solely to the stronger, eastern nation.

Hardly the words of a nationalist (who would have spoken of national renewal and revenge). Yoram Hazony argues that Hitler was a racialist-imperialist rather than a nationalist, because he privileged an Aryan racial empire over the German nation.

During the Cold War, conservative intellectuals, including Straussians and the brilliant Jesuit priest John Courtney Murray, advanced the concept of America as a "proposition nation" that was in conflict with a rival ideological nation, the Soviet Union. This conception of American identity based primarily on shared ideas took hold on the right. However, the translation of creedal doctrine from professors to politicians was often clumsily done and opened the door to utopian interpretations. Thus we have Paul Ryan, while arguing for "comprehensive immigration reform," declaring: "America is more than just a country. It's more than Chicago, or Wisconsin. It's more than our borders. America is an idea. It's a very precious idea."

While conservatives embraced the "nation based on ideas" paradigm, the progressives who control America's universities and schools happily "appropriated" the concept (they never liked all that flag-waving stuff anyway) and filled in the educational content. First, the progressives noted that American "ideals," like the nation itself, were constantly "evolving." Lawrence Levine in *The Opening of the American Mind* declared that America is "continually in process of happening"; it is a "dynamic becoming." Michael Walzer wrote that "America is still a radically unfinished society."

Second, the progressives redefined these ideals as utopian aspirations for leftist social justice to substitute more "advanced" viewpoints for outmoded 18th-century concepts and, in the case of the legal status of marriage, even the thinking of the first-term Obama administration. The Straussians emphasized the ideals of the Declaration, the Constitution, and the *Federalist Papers*. In contrast, Todd Gitlin declared that, while America is the fulfillment of the Enlightenment, "the point is not to celebrate some accomplished Enlightenment," with its "Declaration of Independence" and "its *Federalist Papers* and Constitutional debates," but to see the American project "as an aspiration, an invitation, a commitment to a process that seriously aims to bring about understandings that do not yet exist." Whereas John Courtney Murray in *We Hold These Truths* declared that the "first truth" of the "American Proposition" is that we are a "nation under God," the progressive thinker Richard

Rorty called on Americans to embrace the utopian dreams of Walt Whitman and John Dewey. Whitman and Dewey "wanted that utopian America to replace God as the unconditional object of desire," Rorty told us. "They wanted the struggle for social justice to be the county's animating principle." During his two terms in office, Barack Obama skillfully modulated and popularized the core progressive narrative of American history as the unfolding of a left-oriented social justice.

Conservatives made a strategic mistake overemphasizing abstract ideological reasoning while downplaying the concrete cultural and emotional aspect of patriotism. James Madison himself in *Federalist* No. 49 warned us that even the most "rational" regime is better off with the "prejudices of the community on its side." ("Prejudices" in the 18th-century understanding did not have the negative connotation that it does today and was closer to the concept of "sentiments.")

If patriotism is defined only as the fulfillment of "shared" American ideals (even as the nation becomes more polarized), then it will be neutered and devoid of any emotional attachment to national symbols and national stories. I mean symbols and stories such as Washington crossing the Delaware; the building of the transcontinental railroad; the pioneers on the frontier; the entrepreneurs who created the greatest economy the world has ever known; Gettysburg; the moral force of the civil-rights movement; and the Marines raising the flag on Iwo Jima. If this comes to pass, if patriotism is completely divorced from nationalism, then patriotism itself will be hollowed out, an empty shell.

This is the inevitable result of the "patriotism good, nationalism bad" argument. Anti-nationalism leads to anti-patriotism except for the most cold, abstract variety of what remains of "patriotism," which itself easily becomes a form of utopianism with a progressive bent. And this trajectory, from a historically concrete patriotism and nationalism to a "patriotism" consisting primarily of "striving to fulfill our ideals" of a utopian progressivism, is already happening in our universities and schools. At the end of the day, to paraphrase Ben Franklin, patriotism and nationalism will either hang together, or they will hang separately, both diluted and diminished.

CHAPTER 3

Does the Global Rise of Nationalism Mean the End of Liberal Democracy?

Liberal Democracy at a Global Historical Crossroads

Ganesh Sitaraman

Ganesh Sitaraman is a professor of law at Vanderbilt University and a senior fellow at the Center for American Progress.

Over the past few years, I have frequently been reminded of David Foster Wallace's commencement address at Kenyon College in 2005. Wallace began with the story of two fish swimming together, when an older fish swims by and says "Morning boys, how's the water?" After the old fish swims away, one says to the other, "What the hell is water?"

Over the last year or two, there's been a lot of discussion about what drove Trump voters and Brexit voters to the polls. There's been concern as specific constitutional and political norms break down. But with so many people running from tweet-storm to tweet-storm, there has been comparatively less attention to what happened to the water—to the root causes of the global crisis of democracy.

Yascha Mounk's extraordinary new book, *The People versus Democracy*, provides a clear, concise, persuasive, and insightful account of the conditions that made liberal democracy work – and how the breakdown in those conditions is the source of the current crisis of democracy around the world. He reveals the water in which liberal democracy has been swimming unthinkingly all these years.

The success and stability of liberal democracy, Mounk argues, was premised on three assumptions about social life. First, the citizenry had a relatively similar worldview because broadcast news, newspapers, radio, and the like were all one-to-many forms of communication in which gatekeepers ensured that news and information remained within the mainstream. This meant that even diverse communities were part of a shared conversation based on shared facts.

"The three crises of liberal democracy," by Ganesh Sitaraman, Guardian News & Media Limited, March 17, 2018. Reprinted by permission.

The second assumption was broadly-shared economic growth and relative economic equality. For most of the history of the world, there was basically no economic growth. Only since the dawn of the industrial revolution has growth skyrocketed, meaning that people could aspire to (and expect) higher living standards. And in the few decades after the second world war specifically, growth combined with low levels of economic inequality meaning that the rising tide actually did lift all boats.

The final assumption was social homogeneity. Eras of stable liberal democracies around the world, Mounk argues, have largely been characterized by relatively homogeneous populations. In Europe, for example, the rise of democracy and the breaking of empires—like the polyglot Austro-Hungarian empire—were inextricably tied to nationalism.

In the last generation, and in particular, in the last fifteen or so years, Mounk argues that all three assumptions have come under severe stress. Social media has turned any individual into a broadcaster, and allowed people to hear only the news, facts, and opinions they want to hear. This in turn has expanded the reach of radical and fringe ideas and conspiracy theories. Growth has been stagnant for the average worker for a generation, and people are anxious that their kids' generation will make it financially. Finally, immigration has increased since the mid-twentieth century, sparking racial and cultural anxiety in locations that have seen particularly rapid increases in diversity.

The consequence, Mounk argues, is that liberal democracy is coming apart. On the one side, we see the rise of "illiberal democracies"—governments that claim to represent the "real" people of the nation, but have little regard for individual rights or constitutional norms. Many refer to these movements as populist. At the same time, others flirt with what Mounk calls "undemocratic liberalism," a style of governance which preserves rights but at the expense of democratic engagement and accountability. Think of this as government by elite technocrats who have little faith in ordinary people.

What is so troubling is that these two responses might be mutually reinforcing. Mounk, a lecturer at Harvard University, doesn't make much of this point, but it is worth resting on for a moment. When populists gain power, their opponents are likely to see the virtues of undemocratic liberalism. When undemocratic liberalism gains steam, many ordinary people will feel locked out and that public policies are unresponsive to their demands—pushing them to want to overthrow the elites. In the ensuing cycle, the loser is liberal democracy, which is assaulted for both its liberalism and its democracy.

One of the great strengths of Mounk's book is that he eschews simple, singular explanations—and as a result, easy solutions. Mounk offers three directions to save liberal democracy from its enemies. The most worked out is an economic reform agenda to alleviate the unequal distribution of economic growth and mitigate the insecurity that stems from technology and globalization. The least worked out—perhaps because it is the most difficult —is an agenda to revive "civic faith," our shared set of facts and information, trust in political institutions, and our sense of civic decency. This arena deserves more attention because it is unclear how to achieve policy changes of any kind in a polarized society that has few shared facts and whose civic muscles are atrophying.

The most interesting suggestion, however, might be Mounk's call for imagining a new form of nationalism, which he calls "inclusive nationalism." Instead of responding to the rise of nationalism with its polar opposite, utopian cosmopolitanism, Mounk says we need to "domesticate nationalism," and he offer a vision for an integrated society in which nationalism unites people, rather than divides them.

All three parts of this agenda might seem uncomfortable to those who wish to continue politics as usual. Economic reforms threaten the most powerful people and interest groups in society. Restoring civic faith means breaking out of tribalism in society, politics, and education. Inclusive nationalism challenges the conventional rhetoric on both right and left. But we now swim in more dangerous waters, and we can no longer take the persistence of liberal democracy for granted.

Contemporary Nationalist Movements Represent a Reaction Against Liberal Hegemony

Damon Linker

Damon Linker is an American writer and political analyst. He is a contributing editor for the New Republic *and a senior writing fellow in the Center for Critical Writing at the University of Pennsylvania.*

Three years after the twin shocks of President Trump's triumph in the Republican primaries and the narrow win for "Leave" in the Brexit referendum, the evidence has never been stronger that the world has entered an era of anti-liberalism.

Later this week, voters across Europe go to the polls to vote in EU parliamentary elections that could deliver a quarter or more of the seats to the continent's right-wing populists and nationalists. Meanwhile, exit polls in India suggest that Narendra Modi's Hindu nationalist party will win re-election when results are announced on May 23. This follows the surprise victory in Australia of Scott Morrison's conservative coalition, which leaned heavily on populist themes.

These events follow on the heels of many others. Brazil, Colombia, Italy, Hungary, Poland, Austria, Turkey, Russia, Israel, and Japan are all led by right-wing nationalists or populists, or their governing coalitions include parties firmly in that camp. In many other countries, such parties have been founded and won legislative seats. There is no sign yet that the rising tide has crested, or how high it may go.

But what does the shift amount to? Is it a temporary anomaly that can easily be reversed, as Democratic presidential frontrunner Joe Biden likes to imply? Or is it, as many others warn ominously, a sign that democracy itself is under siege?

"Democracy isn't dying. Liberalism is," by Damon Linker, The Week Publications Inc, May 21, 2019. Reprinted by permission.

Both options are wrong. The trend is far too widespread for it to be the result of a fluke that can be quickly and easily reversed. That doesn't mean that the insurgents won't suffer defeats; Biden or some other Democrat may well beat Trump in 2020. But it does mean that the political challenge posed by Trump and the other populists and nationalists is likely to persist for some time to come.

As for the question that *The New York Review of Books* has plastered across the cover of its most recent issue—"Is democracy dying?"—the answer, quite clearly, is no: Democracy is not in jeopardy. Liberalism is.

It is imperative that we learn to recognize the difference and uphold the distinction. Democracy is nothing more or less than political rule by the people. In ancient Athens, this meant that political offices were allocated by lot: anyone who was a citizen might be called upon to serve. In modern democracies, political offices are won through electoral contests, with the majority or plurality winner of the vote gaining power and serving as a representative of the people.

Liberalism, by contrast, is a modification of government meant to produce balance, fairness, and wisdom. It includes the protection of individual freedoms (rights), an independent judiciary, a free press, and the rule of law, including professional civil servants and bureaucrats who are guided by expertise and a sense of public spiritedness. When these liberal norms and institutions, which aim to regularize and restrain the exercise of government power, are combined with democratic elections, the country is called a liberal democracy. But liberalism can be applied to other forms of government as well.

Whether liberalism is combined with democracy, monarchy, or another form of government, it adds an element of elevation, since it makes distinctions between acceptable and unacceptable uses of government power, good and bad applications of the law, and worthwhile and foolish policy goals. These ongoing acts of ranking and judging place liberalism in tension with contrary political impulses. In a liberal monarchy, the norms and institutions of the liberal state will come into conflict with the will of the king or queen. In a liberal democracy, tensions are more likely to arise between the liberal state and the will of the people, expressed through both elections and public opinion (with the latter measured by opinion polls).

Over the past several decades, this classical understanding of liberalism has become more complicated and muddled, as the center-left and center-right parties that have governed so many of the world's democracies have associated their own constellation of contingent policy preferences with the liberal order itself. To support liberal democratic government as such has meant favoring policies of economic and cultural globalization, including the relatively free movement of people, goods, services, and capital around the globe, along with the practical consequences of those policies, including high rates of immigration, economic growth in cosmopolitan cities with high levels of education, and economic decline in lower-density and rural regions.

The result has been that as political movements have risen up to oppose these policies and their consequences, these movements have not just targeted the politicians and parties that championed them, but "liberalism" itself. And they have done so in the name of democracy.

Such populist appeals are not wholly disingenuous. This can be especially hard to see in the United States, where the Constitution's myriad counter-majoritarian features make it possible for a candidate and party to win the presidency and control of Congress while losing the popular vote. In that context, a populist-nationalist upsurge can take—and in 2016, did take—an anti-democratic form.

But in many other countries, the populists are actually popular. Brexit was approved by a majority. Jair Bolsonaro won the presidency of Brazil with 55 percent of the vote. The populist-nationalist coalition that governs Italy won a solid majority at the polls. The party of the most explicitly and aggressively anti-liberal populist in the world—Viktor Orbán—won Hungary's 2018 election with slightly less than 50 percent, but the runner-up was the even further right-wing Jobbik party with an additional 19 percent.

Across the world, democracy is delivering anti-liberal results. Liberals should be honest about what this means—among other things that they are failing to persuade sufficient numbers of voters to entrust them with power, and that this failure has begun to discredit the very norms and institutions that make our democracies liberal in the broader and deeper sense. The result is likely to be a spike in corruption and a decline in freedom for everyone who isn't owed a favor by the ruling party.

How liberals might do a better job of persuading increasingly hostile voters to give them continued, or a renewed, chance at power is anyone's guess. What's not mysterious is how counter-productive it is when liberals respond to popular opposition by lashing out in condescension at the those who withhold their support. Whether such condescension takes the form of an epithet ("deplorables") or an insinuation that voters are too stupid to recognize the wisdom of casting ballots for politicians who promise to enact liberal policies, it wounds pride and triggers a sense of dishonor among voters that can ensure a deepening of hostility to liberalism.

Liberalism and democracy have gone together for a long time. But there's no guarantee the pairing will last—or that they can easily be brought back into alignment once the ties between them have been severed.

Liberal Democracy in Decline

Council on Foreign Relations

The Council on Foreign Relations (CFR) is a nonpartisan membership organization, think tank, and publisher focused on international politics and economics. CFR's flagship publication Foreign Affairs *has long been among America's leading forums for serious discussion of international topics.*

Centralization of power in the executive, politicization of the judiciary, attacks on independent media, the use of public office for private gain—the signs of democratic regression are well known. The only surprising thing is where they've turned up," writes Editor Gideon Rose in his introduction to the May/June issue of *Foreign Affairs*. "As a Latin American friend put it ruefully, 'We've seen this movie before, just never in English.'" The issue's lead package, "*Is Democracy Dying?*," puts the country's current troubles into historical and international perspective.

"There is now a pervasive sense of despair about American democracy," writes Bard College Professor Walter Russell Mead. But, reflecting on the transformation, social upheaval, and political failure in the decades following the end of the U.S. Civil War, Mead notes that United States failed its way to success then, and can do so again. "Humans are problem-solving animals. We thrive on challenges," he writes. "The good news and the bad news are perhaps the same: the American people, in common with others around the world, have the opportunity to reach unimaginable levels of affluence and freedom."

"The long century during which Western liberal democracies dominated the globe has ended for good," write Harvard University lecturer Yascha Mounk and University of Melbourne lecturer Roberto Stefan Foa. They argue that such governments have gotten worse at delivering economic growth, whereas authoritarian states have gotten better at doing so. "The only remaining question now is whether democracy will transcend its once firm anchoring in the West, a shift that would create the conditions for a truly global democratic century—or whether democracy will become, at best, the lingering form of government in an economically and demographically declining corner of the world."

"The immediate cause of rising support for authoritarian, xenophobic populist movements is a reaction against immigration (and, in the United States, rising racial equality)," observes University of Michigan Professor Ronald Inglehart. He warns that the world is experiencing the most severe democratic setback since the rise of fascism in the 1930s. "But all is not lost. Today's democratic decline can be reversed," he writes, "if rich countries address the growing inequality of recent decades and manage the transition to the automated economy."

While most pundits argue that China has bucked the traditional path of modernization by making economic reforms but not political ones, University of Michigan Associate Professor Yuen Yuen Ang argues that "China has in fact pursued significant political reforms—just not in the manner that Western observers expected." Describing China as an "autocracy with democratic characteristics," she catalogues many behind-the-scenes bureaucratic reforms that have not delivered political freedom but that have made the government more responsive. She cautions, however, that "As prosperity continues to increase and demands on the bureaucracy grow, the limits of this approach are beginning to loom large."

"Eastern European populism is a recent phenomenon, but it has deep roots in the region's politics and is unlikely to go away anytime soon," writes Centre for Liberal Strategies' Chair Ivan Krastev. He outlines how the demographic changes that followed the 1989 revolutions—namely, the departure of "the most educated and liberal eastern Europeans"—set the stage for the region's current democratic backsliding in Hungary, Poland, and elsewhere. Writing of voters' embrace of illiberal democracy, he laments, "What makes it particularly dangerous is that it is an authoritarianism born within the framework of democracy itself."

"Xi [Jinping] has matched the dramatic growth of his personal power with an equally dramatic intensification of the Chinese Communist Party's power in society and the economy," writes CFR Senior Fellow Elizabeth C. Economy, author of *The Third Revolution: Xi Jinping and the New Chinese State*, in a detailed portrait of China's ambitious leader. "For the foreseeable future, then, the United States will have to deal with China as it is: an illiberal state seeking to reshape the international system in its own image."

The opioid crisis, once confined mostly to the United States, is starting to go global, raising the specter of "a global opioid epidemic," warn Stanford University's Keith Humphreys, Carnegie Mellon University's Jonathan P. Caulkins, and Brookings Institution's Vanda Felbab-Brown. "Yet in the face of this terrifying possibility, the world has remained largely complacent. Governments and international organizations urgently need to learn the lessons of the North American crisis," they write, calling for greater regulation of the sale and marketing of opioids. A global pandemic is avoidable, "but only if the world's governments stop sleepwalking toward disaster."

Texas A&M University's F. Gregory Gause III notes that Saudi Crown Prince Mohammed bin Salman's "concentrated authority and evident will to shake up the system make it possible for him to do great things. But he has also removed the restraints that have made Saudi foreign and domestic policy cautious, conservative, and ultimately successful amid the crises of the modern Middle East." Gause also asks "whether the crown prince can pull off his high-stakes gamble . . . without destabilizing his country and adding to the region's chaos."

"When it comes to North Korea, U.S. President Donald Trump's policies have been whiplash inducing," argue Georgetown University Professor Victor Cha and Center for Strategic and International Studies' Fellow Katrin Fraser Katz, who lay out a fresh strategy to coerce Pyongyang. "Trump's newfound enthusiasm for diplomacy has temporarily lowered the temperature on the Korean Peninsula, but it also underlines a bigger question: Does the United States have a strategy for North Korea, or are these twists and turns merely the whims of a temperamental president?"

"North Korea has all but completed its quest for nuclear weapons" and "the result is a new, more dangerous phase in the U.S.–North Korean relationship: a high-stakes nuclear standoff," observe Columbia University's Robert Jervis and Yale Law School's Mira Rapp-Hooper. "Regardless of whether diplomacy proceeds or the United States turns its focus to other tools—sanctions, deterrence, even military force—the same underlying challenge will remain: the outcome of this standoff will be determined by whether and how each country can influence the other."

A Global Picture of the Recession of Democracy

Freedom House

Freedom House is an independent watchdog organization dedicated to the expansion of freedom and democracy around the world.

Democracy is under assault and in retreat around the globe, a crisis that has intensified as America's democratic standards erode at an accelerating pace, according to *Freedom in the World 2018*, the latest edition of the annual report on political rights and civil liberties, released today by Freedom House.

The report finds that 2017 was the 12th consecutive year of decline in global freedom. Seventy-one countries suffered net declines in political rights and civil liberties in 2017, with only 35 registering gains. Once-promising states such as Turkey, Venezuela, Poland, and Tunisia were among those experiencing declines in democratic standards. The recent democratic opening in Myanmar was permanently damaged by a shocking campaign of ethnic cleansing against the Rohingya minority.

"Democracy is facing its most serious crisis in decades," said Michael J. Abramowitz, president of Freedom House. "Democracy's basic tenets—including guarantees of free and fair elections, the rights of minorities, freedom of the press, and the rule of law—are under siege around the world."

Freedom in the World 2018 reports on how China and Russia have taken advantage of the retreat of leading democracies both to increase repression at home and to export their malign influence to other countries. To maintain power, these autocratic regimes are acting beyond their borders to squelch open debate, pursue dissidents, and compromise rules-based institutions.

"Democracy in Crisis: Freedom House Releases Freedom in the World 2018," Freedom House, January 16, 2018. Reprinted by permission.

A major development of 2017 was the retreat of the United States as both a champion and an exemplar of democracy. While Freedom House has tracked a slow decline in political rights and civil liberties in the United States for the past seven years, the decline accelerated in 2017, owing to growing evidence of Russian interference in the 2016 elections, violations of basic ethical standards by the new administration, and a reduction in government transparency.

Although U.S. institutions like the press and the judiciary have remained resilient in the face of unprecedented attacks from President Trump, the attacks could ultimately leave them weakened, with serious implications for the health of U.S. democracy and America's place in the world. Meanwhile, the abdication of the traditional U.S. role as the leading champion of democracy is of deep concern and potential consequence in the ongoing struggle against modern authoritarians and their pernicious ideas.

"The core institutions of American democracy are being battered by an administration that has treated the country's traditional checks and balances with disdain," Abramowitz said.

"The Trump administration has made a sharp break from the political consensus of the last 70 years by casting aside democracy as the animating force behind American foreign policy," Abramowitz added. "The hastening withdrawal of the United States from its historical commitment to supporting democracy overseas makes the challenge posed by authoritarian regimes all the more powerful and threatening."

In another significant development, Turkey moved from Partly Free to Not Free as President Recep Tayyip Erdoğan broadened and intensified the crackdown on his perceived opponents that began after a failed 2016 coup attempt, with dire consequences for Turkish citizens.

Over the period since the 12-year slide began in 2006, 113 countries have seen a net decline, and only 62 have experienced a net improvement.

Key Global Findings

- Of the 195 countries assessed, 88 (45 percent) were rated Free, 58 (30 percent) Partly Free, and 49 (25 percent) Not Free.
- The United States saw declines in its political rights due to:
  - Growing evidence of Russian interference in the 2016 election campaign and a lack of action by the Trump administration either to condemn or to prevent a reoccurrence of such meddling.
  - Violations of basic ethical standards by the new administration, including the president's failure to divest himself of his business empire, his hiring of family members as senior advisers, and his appointment of cabinet members and other senior officials despite apparent conflicts of interest.
  - A reduction in government transparency, including an unusual pattern of false statements by the administration, the president's failure to disclose basic information such as his personal tax data, policy and other decisions made without meaningful input from relevant agencies and officials, and the removal of information on issues of public interest from government websites for political or ideological reasons.
- Corrupt and repressive states such as Saudi Arabia, Iran, Venezuela, and North Korea put global stability at risk by perpetuating long-running regional conflicts, fueling humanitarian crises, and in North Korea's case, rapidly expanding its nuclear arsenal.
- Sharp democratic declines in Tunisia in 2017 threatened the only Free country in the Arab world and the sole success story from the 2011 Arab Spring.

- The forced resignation under military pressure of elected president Robert Mugabe pushed Zimbabwe over the threshold from Partly Free to Not Free.
- Myanmar's campaign of ethnic cleansing in 2017 demonstrated the flawed nature of the country's limited democratic opening, which had been welcomed by the international community since 2010.

The Worst of the Worst

Of the 49 countries designated as Not Free, the following 12 have the worst aggregate scores for political rights and civil liberties, earning less than 10 points on a 100-point scale (beginning with the least free): Syria, South Sudan, Eritrea, North Korea, Turkmenistan, Equatorial Guinea, Saudi Arabia, Somalia, Uzbekistan, Sudan, Central African Republic, and Libya.

Key Regional Findings

Americas

- Under new president Lenín Moreno, Ecuador unexpectedly turned away from repressive rule, easing pressure on the media, promoting greater engagement with civil society, and supporting anticorruption efforts.
- Mexico's democracy has been shaken by new revelations of extensive state surveillance aimed at journalists and civil society activists who threatened to expose government corruption and other wrongdoing.

Asia

- Hong Kong's diminishing political rights received another blow as four prodemocracy lawmakers were expelled from the legislature, protest leaders were sentenced to jail time, and pro-Beijing authorities worked to stamp out a movement calling for local self-determination.

- The Communist Party leadership in Beijing continued to expand its international influence by building up a propaganda and censorship apparatus with global reach. It used economic and other ties to influence democracies like Australia and New Zealand, compelled various countries to repatriate Chinese citizens seeking refuge abroad, and provided diplomatic and material support to repressive governments from Southeast Asia to Africa.
- Hopes for democracy in Cambodia were dashed as Prime Minister Hun Sen oversaw a decisive crackdown on the country's beleaguered opposition and press corps.
- Nepal held its first national, regional, and local elections under a new constitution, with high voter turnout despite some reports of violence.

Eurasia

- Vladimir Putin's Russia demonstrated the increasing sophistication and reach of modern authoritarian regimes. It organized disinformation campaigns during elections in European democracies, cultivated ties with xenophobic political parties across the continent, threatened its closest neighbors, and served as an alternative source of military aid for Middle Eastern dictatorships. A central goal of these efforts was to disrupt democratic states and fracture the institutions that bind them together.
- Surrounded by neighbors with entrenched dictators, Uzbekistan prompted cautious optimism as its new administration—formed after the death of longtime autocrat Islam Karimov—ended some forms of forced labor and granted new if limited space for civil society.

Europe

- In Hungary and Poland, populist leaders continued to consolidate power, smearing the opposition in public media and passing laws designed to curb civil society. Poland's ruling party also pressed ahead with an alarming effort to assert political control over the judiciary.
- Reverberations from the 2015–16 refugee crisis continued to fuel the rise of xenophobic, far-right parties, which gained ground in elections in France, Germany, the Netherlands, and Austria.
- In Serbia, EU leaders' tolerance of President Aleksandar Vučić's authoritarian tendencies allowed him to further sideline the opposition and undermine what remains of the country's independent media.

Middle East and North Africa

- Libya slid into the Worst of the Worst category as disputes between rival authorities in the country's east and west led to political paralysis. Reports of modern-day slave markets were added to other abuses against refugees and migrants stranded in militia-run detention camps.
- In Saudi Arabia, Crown Prince Mohammed bin Salman announced plans for social and economic reforms, but he also presided over hundreds of arbitrary arrests and aggressive moves against potential rivals. He showed no inclination to open the political system.

Sub-Saharan Africa

- The forced exit of President Robert Mugabe in late 2017 left the future of democracy in Zimbabwe uncertain, given that his successor was a key member of Mugabe's repressive regime.
- While Kenya's Supreme Court initially won broad praise for annulling the results of what it deemed to be a flawed presidential election, President Uhuru Kenyatta's ultimate

victory in a rerun was marred by a lack of substantive electoral reforms, incidents of political violence, and a boycott by the main opposition candidate.

- In Tanzania, the government of President John Magufuli stepped up repression of dissent, detaining opposition politicians, shuttering media outlets, and arresting citizens for posting critical views on social media.
- In a rare positive story, The Gambia secured one of the largest improvements to date in *Freedom in the World.* The West African state moved from Not Free to Partly Free after former dictator Yahya Jammeh—under international pressure—finally conceded to elected president Adama Barrow, leading to successful legislative elections, a return of exiled journalists and activists, and the release of political prisoners.

Countries to Watch in 2018

The following countries are among those that may experience important developments in the coming year, and deserve special scrutiny.

- Opposition alliances are crystallizing ahead of Afghanistan's long-overdue parliamentary elections, but preparations for the polls have been lacking, and it is uncertain whether they will be held as planned in 2018.
- Newly elected President João Lourenço of Angola moved to weaken the control of his predecessor's family in 2017, but it remains to be seen whether he will make a serious effort to stem endemic corruption or ease restrictions on politics, the media, and civil society.
- The ruling Georgian Dream party recently pushed through constitutional amendments in Georgia that—combined with the financial backing of its reclusive billionaire patron—will make an effective challenge by the fractured opposition in future elections even more unlikely, potentially cementing the party's control for years to come.

- Improved security in Iraq has enabled competition among newly registered parties and candidates ahead of the 2018 elections, which will test the resilience of the country's political system.
- A democratically elected, ethnically inclusive government in Macedonia is seeking to root out corruption and other systemic abuses that grew worse under its scandal-plagued predecessor.
- The July 2018 general elections in Mexico will serve as a referendum on an administration that has failed to curb rampant violence and corruption, and has become increasingly hostile toward independent media and civil society activists.
- Crown Prince Mohammed bin Salman's controversial reform program in Saudi Arabia is likely to cause even more upheaval in government and society, as small gains in social freedoms and efforts to attract foreign investors go hand in hand with attempts to quash dissent and fight off perceived opponents.
- Under new leadership, South Africa's African National Congress will be under pressure to clean up its image—sullied by corruption linked to President Jacob Zuma—ahead of general elections in 2019.
- The media and the judiciary in the United States—both of which have a long history of independence—face acute pressure from the Trump administration, whose smears threaten to undermine their legitimacy.
- Uzbekistan's new government has taken tentative steps toward greater openness and international engagement, but lasting change in one of the world's most repressive political systems will require sustained international attention as well as support for independent voices in the country's media and civil society.

The West Is in an Age of Retreat

Mark Triffitt

Mark Triffitt is a lecturer in the School of Social and Political Sciences at the University of Melbourne in Australia. He is a former political and policy advisor to governments and corporations.

When future historians look back at our current times how will they define it?

Perhaps they'll see it as a time of geopolitical shifts spurred by the rise of China, or maybe a period of fast technological change driving social and economic upheaval.

They might instead focus on the populist dislocations now battering liberal politics and name it the Era of Trumpism.

But when future historians join the dots from a vantage point of fifty or hundred years from now, they are likely to ponder a central question:

How did the Western liberal world—less than 30 years after declaring itself unassailable as the vanguard of global progress following communism's collapse—find itself in serious retreat from its own core tenets?

Three Forms of Retreat

That the West is now in what I call an "Age of Retreat" is evident in the way it is turning back from its own aspirations; in the barricades it is putting up behind it; and in its intensifying nostalgia for past certainties.

When the Soviet Union collapsed in the early 1990s, the West predicted that democracy and free market systems would spread triumphantly across the globe to fill the vacuum left by communism.

In this post-communist world (where everyone was now a democratic citizen and a free marketeer) it was believed that both democracy and the free market would function more optimally than ever before.

Today, nothing could be further from the truth.

Rather than becoming a gold standard around which 21st century political systems should be organised, Western-style democracy worldwide is now in various stages of retreat.

Nations, like Poland and Hungary, for example, that threw off autocratic shackles and embraced democracy in the 1990s are retreating into quasi-authoritarian rule where free speech is curtailed, elections tainted and human rights abused.

More significantly, in core West democracies like the United States and Australia, democracy's credibility among its own citizens has fallen to historic lows according to surveys.

Orwellian Markets

Democracy's emerging legitimacy crisis is underlined by survey evidence that younger generations across the West are looking increasingly favourably upon authoritarianism as a more 'effective' way to manage the 21st century.

Liberal free markets, on the surface, may seem more progressive than ever in terms of empowering individual freedom and choice. But underneath lies the growing ascendency of digital-driven "surveillance capitalism."

In effect, citizens are being reduced to "data factories" whose private movements, thoughts and behaviour are covertly stalked and monetarised into 'products.'

As a result of this Orwellian turn, markets are shattering individual privacy and autonomy—both cornerstones of Western liberalism.

The primacy of the individual is likewise regressing in terms of the economic opportunities open to people. Across Western market economies, social mobility—a key marker of individual progress—has stalled or gone backwards over the past three decades.

At the same time levels of wealth disparity have accelerated since the Global Financial Crisis of 2007-09, and increasing numbers of Western citizens are being locked out of economic growth.

Significantly, America—once the epicentre of "opportunity for all"—is now regressing into an economic caste system.

Digital Failure

The advent of the internet—alongside the spread of democracy and markets—was hailed as the torch-bearer of Western values in the 1990s. Its unprecedented capacity to connect and inform led many to predict it would enrich political and social debate, creating more respectful deliberation and generally drive a far more vibrant and inclusive public sphere.

Yet, the dream of a digital eco-system that represents the best of Enlightenment ideals is effectively dead.

Instead, by monopolising control of it, a handful of tech titans have profoundly reversed the internet's promise, turning it into a stamping ground for anti-science, hate-based tribalism and fake news.

The second form of retreat sees the West constructing a succession of walls to barricade itself from the world. President Trump's ambitions to build a physical wall to barricade the US from Mexico is already mirrored in the wire fences that now snake their way around Europe's eastern borders.

But these walls are also economic, taking the form of increased protectionism.

They are also cultural, reflecting the growing support for anti-immigration and white-centric racism, particularly in Europe.

The third retreat is psychological.

Retreating Minds

Western politics is increasingly characterised by the rise of extreme right-wing parties evoking the language of ultra-nationalism. An analysis of European elections suggest support for radical right parties is now the highest since the collapse of communism.

Beneath this rise is a mental retreat that hankers for the 'lost paradises' of last century as a refuge from a disorientating present.

All this isn't to say progress hasn't been made. The spread of democracy since the 1990s has disseminated values of freedom and choice. But any clear-eyed view reveals a West increasingly defined by seismic reversals, not advances.

Given tens of thousands of scientists across the world have felt the need over the past two years to march in support of rational thinking and fact-based evidence, it is difficult not to be concerned that we are retreating into a form of De-Enlightenment.

And when the US elects a President who personifies liberalism's new Dark Ages, that retreat looks to have gone mainstream.

What Now?

The reason for the West's unravelling in such a short space of time may not appear to lend itself to easy explanation. But perhaps the reason might be deceptively simple.

Democracy and free markets evolved in the 18th and 19th centuries to steer society through a far less complex, far more predictable economic and political world than today's.

Rapid accelerations and disruptions in the scale, speed and complexity of contemporary life over the last 20 years have challenged many of the baseline assumptions that democracy and markets rely on to organise and steer the world according to "liberal" values and practices.

Maybe, as Western democracies in particular struggle to decipher and organise the 'new normal' of a fundamentally changed and more complex 21st century world they cannot help but retreat into illiberalism.

If this is the case then The Age of Retreat is an urgent wake-up call.

It tells us we need to fundamentally rethink and re-tool our democratic and market systems if they are to again advance liberal practices and values.

Democracy needs to give citizens a bigger, more direct say in public policy making, and in this way restore engagement and legitimacy. Free markets need far more proactive intervention to aggressively tackle corrosive inequality. Internet giants need to be broken up so the digital sphere is re-opened to more players and more competition.

The alternative is a Western world that, far from being a bastion of progress, becomes increasingly a reactionary and retreating garrison of disillusion.

Long-Term Trends Will Prevail over Liberal Democracy's Recent Setbacks

Marc Plattner

Marc Plattner is vice president of research and studies at the National Endowment for Democracy and founding editor of the Journal of Democracy. *His books include* Global Challenges to Liberal Democracy *and* The Global Resurgence of Democracy.

Since the publication of its inaugural issue in January 1990, the *Journal of Democracy* has published well over a thousand articles, exploring all aspects of the workings of democracy and the struggles of democratic movements. But we have been especially concerned with tracking democracy's advances and setbacks around the world. For 25 years, we have been "taking the temperature" of democracy. Since 1998, we have published annually an article summarizing Freedom House's survey of Freedom in the World, and we have featured numerous other essays analyzing democracy's global trajectory, beginning with Samuel P. Huntington's classic 1991 article introducing the concept of the "third wave" of democratization. So it should not be unexpected that we turn to this subject as the central theme of our twenty-fifth anniversary issue.

Some may be surprised, however, by the headline on our cover— "Is Democracy in Decline?"—which faithfully reflects the way in which we posed the question to our contributors. For a journal that is unabashedly in favor of democracy, this obviously is not the kind of celebratory theme that might be preferred for marking a historic milestone. Yet this seemed to be the question that everyone was asking as 2015 approached, and we decided that it deserved a thorough examination.

Tracing the viewpoints and opinions expressed over the years in the *Journal* (especially on its five-year anniversaries) suggests how evaluations of and sentiments about the state of democracy have evolved since 1990. The editors' introduction that Larry Diamond and I wrote for the inaugural issue was animated by the view that democracy was experiencing a "remarkable worldwide resurgence," but also by a concern that it lagged behind its rivals with respect to political ideas and organization. Five eventful years later, we recognized not only that democracy had spread to many more countries but also that it had hugely improved its standing in terms of ideas and organization. We asserted that democracy had "gained enormous ground" with respect to "international legitimacy" and that it now "reign[ed] supreme in the ideological sphere." Multilateral organizations were increasingly endorsing democratic principles, and a whole new field of international democracy assistance had emerged. At the turn of the century, these trends seemed only to be growing stronger. In introducing a special tenth-anniversary issue on "Democracy in the World" modeled on Alexis de Tocqueville's *Democracy in America*, we argued that Tocqueville had supplanted Marx and concluded, "We are all Tocquevilleans now."

By 2005, however, our tone had grown far more downbeat, and we acknowledged a darkening mood among supporters of democracy. We attributed this in part to the travails of democracy-building in postinvasion Iraq and to Russia's descent back into authoritarianism, but argued that the overall global trends were mixed and did not justify discouragement among democrats. By 2010, we were prepared to grant that "there now may even be grounds for speaking of an erosion of freedom over the past few years, though its dimensions are very slight."

Confronting Decline

Yet here in our twenty-fifth anniversary issue, we feel compelled to confront head-on the question of whether democracy is in decline. Why? There are two aspects to the answer, which although intertwined are in some measure separable. The first deals with what is actually taking place on the ground: How many countries are democratic? Is their number rising or shrinking? What is the situation with respect to such liberal-democratic features as freedom of the press, rule of law, free and fair elections, and the like? The second, more subjective, aspect concerns the standing of democracy in the world: How is it viewed in terms of legitimacy and attractiveness? It is in this latter dimension that the evidence, or at least the widespread perception, of decline is most striking.

As readers will see, the first dimension is open to differing interpretations. The divergence among them is most sharply posed by comparing Steven Levitsky and Lucan Way's essay on "The Myth of Democratic Recession" with Larry Diamond's on the need for "Facing Up to the Democratic Recession." Levitsky and Way point out that even the Freedom House data show only a very slight decline in levels of freedom since 2000 and that other indices show none at all. In addition, they argue that during the 1990s most observers (including Freedom House) were too prone to count any country where an autocratic regime fell as a case of transition to democracy. In the view of Levitsky and Way, many of these countries temporarily enjoyed "pluralism by default" because of authoritarian weakness, but never truly established democracy. Many of them have now seen a consolidation of authoritarianism, but because their regimes were wrongly classified as democratic in the first place, this should not be seen as evidence of democratic decline.

Larry Diamond, while not necessarily disputing Levitsky and Way's criticism of how these countries were rated in the early 1990s, finds other empirical evidence that the past decade has been "a period of at least incipient decline in democracy." He cites an increasing incidence of democratic breakdowns, the poor performance of new democracies according to various measures of good governance and rule of law, and democratic backsliding or stagnation in the biggest and wealthiest non-Western countries. There are strong arguments on both sides of this debate, but ultimately I do not think that analyses of the Freedom House (or other) numbers can settle the larger question.

Moreover, the broad contours of the trends revealed by the data are not really in dispute. Democracy began to make significant gains in the world in the years 1975–85. It then advanced at a prodigious rate in 1985–95. Its progress then began to slow, and only modest gains were achieved in the following decade, with scores peaking sometime in the early 2000s. Since then, the pattern has been one of stasis or very minor decline—certainly nothing like the "reverse waves" that Huntington identified in previous eras. The absence of democratic progress can be characterized negatively as "stagnation" or more hopefully as the conserving of prior democratic gains. But even if one discerns in the data a slight fall in the number of democracies, this cannot account for the perception of decline that has been spreading among democracy's friends, foes, and skeptics alike.

In my view, then, we must look elsewhere for the real sources of "declinist" sentiment about democracy, and several of the essays in this issue can help us to locate them. A number of these sources are introduced in the latter part of Larry Diamond's article. One, which Diamond labels "bad governance," is elaborated in the essay by Francis Fukuyama. This term refers in the first instance to the failure of many new democracies to build effective modern states. Because of this failure, which can lead to lagging economic growth, poor public services, lack of personal security, and pervasive corruption, the citizens of such countries understandably feel disappointed by democracy. Fukuyama contends that "the legitimacy of many democracies around the world depends less on the deepening of their democratic institutions than on their ability to provide high-quality governance." Of course, bad governance afflicts most (though not all) nondemocratic countries as well, but this offers scant consolation to citizens who feel that their government is failing them.

Fukuyama concludes that those who wish to strengthen democracy need to pay greater attention to state-building, including such prosaic matters as public administration and policy implementation. This is no doubt useful advice. Yet good governance remain stubbornly hard to achieve, especially in new democracies. In such settings, where citizens are still new to democratic attitudes and institutions, there is an almost inevitable tendency to blame poor governance on democracy. This accounts, at least in part, for democracy's tendency to break down in countries that have adopted it for the first time, and its failure to take root in some places until it has been tried several times. Yet this pattern need not portend democratic failure in the long term. Many more years might be needed to attain democratic consolidation, but time would still be on the side of democracy.

Three Sources of Doubt About Democracy

This optimistic long-term scenario, however, presupposes that democracy remains the goal that countries are seeking. And this in turn is likely to depend on its being viewed both as the global standard of political legitimacy and as the best system for achieving the kind of prosperity and effective governance that almost all countries seek. What has changed most dramatically in recent years is that these presuppositions are increasingly being called into question. In my view, there are three chief reasons for this shift: 1) the growing sense that the advanced democracies are in trouble in terms of their economic and political performance; 2) the new self-confidence and seeming vitality of some authoritarian countries; and 3) the shifting geopolitical balance between the democracies and their rivals.

The first of these was generated by the 2008 financial crisis and its lingering economic consequences, including the recession and high unemployment rates that still plague much of Europe. That the advanced democracies suffered these reverses at a time when emerging-market countries were growing at a rapid clip undercut the notion that the institutions and policies of the West were worthy of emulation by "the rest." The political dysfunction that afflicted the advanced democracies as they sought to respond to the crisis further weakened their appeal. As Thomas Carothers notes in his essay on the changing global context of democracy promotion, "Democracy's travails in both the United States and

Europe have greatly damaged the standing of democracy in the eyes of many people around the world."

The flip side of democracy's dwindling prestige has been the growing clout of a number of leading authoritarian regimes. Key among them is China, whose ability to make enormous economic strides without introducing democratic reforms has cast doubt on the notion that democracy is the only appropriate political system for wealthy countries. At the same time, as E. Gyimah-Boadi points out, China "is providing African governments with alternative non-Western markets, trade partners, and sources of military and development aid"—aid that is not tied to considerations of human rights or government accountability in the recipient states. Nor is China the only assertive nondemocratic power. Russia, Iran, Saudi Arabia, and Venezuela also have been learning from one another and even cooperating directly to thwart democracy's progress.

The essay on China in this issue by Andrew J. Nathan is the first in a series that the *Journal of Democracy* will be publishing in 2015 on what we have labeled the "authoritarian resurgence." It hurts to use this title; our first *Journal of Democracy* book, published in 1993, was called *The Global Resurgence of Democracy*. But today it does seem to be authoritarianism that has the wind at its back, even if it has not yet spread to many more countries. One sign of this is the headway that the authoritarians have made in the realm of "soft power," especially in major regional and multilateral organizations. The prodemocratic norms that the democracies helped to embed in organizations such as the OSCE, the Council of Europe, and the OAS in the 1990s are being weakened by antidemocratic nations represented in these bodies. Countries such as Russia and China also are ramping up their cultural diplomacy and international broadcasting while Western efforts in these fields have been unfocused and underfunded.

But it is not only in "soft-power" competition that the advanced democracies have fallen short. Increasingly, they are looking weaker in terms of hard power as well, shrinking their defense budgets even as authoritarian states spend more on arms. Over the past 25 years, the *Journal of Democracy* devoted little attention to issues of interstate relations or military affairs. In part, this reflected our sense of where the *Journal* enjoys a comparative advantage among world-affairs periodicals—most of them focus on security and foreign policy, while few study the domestic politics of non-Western countries. But we also felt that the internal developments accompanying or preceding struggles over democracy often were decisive in shaping the direction of international relations. Certainly that seemed true during the height of the third wave. Though the international context mattered, of course, the spark for change frequently came from internal grievances, movements, and conflicts, and by concentrating on these the *Journal*, in our view, was generally "ahead of the curve" in providing insight into how international developments would unfold.

We still think that the focus we have chosen is the right one for the *Journal*, but I have begun to wonder whether the period of the 1990s was atypical. Perhaps the "unipolar moment" of overwhelming dominance by the United States and its democratic allies had made it possible for internal prodemocratic struggles to take center stage, and without this favorable international environment democracy would not have prospered. This is certainly the interpretation suggested by Robert Kagan in this issue. As he puts it, "Geopolitical shifts among the reigning great powers, often but not always the result of wars, can have a significant effect on the domestic politics of the smaller and weaker nations of the world." Kagan asserts that the United States is in "a state of retrenchment" in the international arena, and that this is inflicting "collateral damage" on the fortunes of democracy.

In 2014, these trends became manifest. The rise of ISIS in Syria and Iraq, amid the disappointed hopes of the "Arab Spring" (outside Tunisia) and worries about Afghanistan, made it clear, as Tarek Masoud underlines, that Western efforts to impose some kind of order and to encourage democracy in the broader Middle East were not succeeding. Meanwhile, China's muscle-flexing in the East and South China Seas seemed to fore- shadow a return to the use of force in Asia. And most important of all, Russia's brazen annexation of Crimea and stealth invasion of eastern Ukraine showed that the rules-based international order built by democratic powers could no longer be taken for granted. Moreover, if Lilia Shevtsova is right in her analysis of Russia's political system, "the Kremlin will henceforth approach the outside world in a militarist mode, with any compromises limited to the realm of tactics and not meant to be lasting."

If the liberal world order is indeed coming apart under pressure from the authoritarians, the future of democracy will be deeply affected. In a globe divided into spheres of influence and power blocs, a country's ability to follow a democratic path will be determined above all by its international alliances and its geography. As Alina Mungiu-Pippidi points out, it increasingly looks as if the fate of democracy in the countries of the postcommunist world will depend on which side of the emerging border between Russia and the EU they find themselves.

This new salience of geopolitics threatens to change the rules of the game. It may both limit the centrality of the internal balance of forces in shaping a country's regime choices and increase the chances that the imposition of external force will be decisive. Moreover, if the geopolitical balance appears to be tilting the authoritarians' way, they will seem much more attractive to the many individuals and nations that seek above all to be on the stronger side. Under these conditions, democracy would lose much of its luster. Where it broke down, there would be less demand to restore it. One could no longer be confident that time would still be on democracy's side.

This gloomy scenario is far from being foreordained. The authoritarians have many weaknesses (which will grow if the recent oil-price drop persists), and democracy has many strengths, including the capacity for self-correction. Though it is often complacent and slow to move, democracy also has shown a remarkable ability to respond to crises. It was arguably in deeper trouble in the 1970s than it is today, but it bounced back. It can do so again. But first its supporters must undertake a clear-eyed appraisal of its current decline and summon the resolve and seriousness of purpose needed to reverse it.

Liberal Democracy Is Resilient and Adaptable

Steven Pinker and Robert Muggah

Steven Pinker is a cognitive psychologist and linguist by training who has written extensively on topics ranging from evolutionary psychology to democratic politics. Robert Muggah is a Canadian political scientist and co-founder of the Igarapé Institute and the SecDev Foundation.

Although democracy has spread from one country to more than 100 countries in the space of two centuries, it has also suffered setbacks along the way, and continues to face resistance to this day. Democracy, after all, is not inevitable, and yet it remains the best system of governance compared to the known alternatives.

Though some countries (and cities) are faring worse than others, the world is becoming safer and more prosperous overall—hard as that may be to believe. This is especially true of democratic countries, which stand out for their higher rates of economic growth and higher levels of wellbeing. Democracies also tend to have fewer wars and genocides, virtually no famines, and happier, healthier, better-educated citizens.

The good news is that a sizeable majority of the world's population now lives in a democracy. Yet in some of them—not least the United States—the rise of populist, nativist political parties and leaders with authoritarian tendencies has created an unmistakable sense of pessimism, leading many to fear for the future of democracy. Are people right to be worried?

Democratic Sea Change

Many people forget that liberal democracy is a relatively new idea. Most of its core precepts—the separation of powers, human rights, civil liberties, freedom of speech and assembly, pluralistic media,

"Is Liberal Democracy in Retreat?" by Steven Pinker and Robert Muggah, Project Syndicate, March 30, 2018. Reprinted by permission.

and free, fair, and competitive elections—did not genuinely take hold until the twentieth century. Until a few hundred years ago, most societies had swung between anarchy and various forms of tyranny.

Governments before the modern era brought about only marginal improvements in the lives of their subjects, whom they often kept in check through brutal repression. Ruthless despotism endured in most places, because the alternative—a Hobbesian state of anarchy—was even worse. The emergence of democracy was far from inevitable.

In fact, the spread of democratic governments after the eighteenth century was a rather stop-start affair. According to the late Harvard University political scientist Samuel P. Huntington, it came in three waves. The first began in the nineteenth century, led by the US, which had developed a system of constitutional democracy that was widely admired for its checks on executive, legislative, and judicial power and privilege. Throughout the nineteenth century, Western European countries, in particular, emulated the US model. By 1922, there were some 29 democracies in existence around the world, though that number would fall to 12 by 1942.

The second wave, according to Huntington, came after the Allied victory in World War II, and crested in 1962, when there were 36 democracies around the world. Again, the wave would ebb somewhat. By 1975, the number had fallen to 30, owing to communist takeovers and pushback from authoritarian regimes in Europe, Latin America, Africa, the Middle East, and Southeast Asia.

The third wave was more of a tsunami. Military and fascist governments fell left, right, and center throughout the 1970s and 1980s. After the fall of the Berlin Wall in 1989 and the implosion of the Soviet Union in 1991, the number of democracies worldwide effectively tripled. By the start of US President Barack Obama's administration in 2009, there were 87 democracies worldwide.

Marching Backward

Looking back, the immediate post-Cold War period seems like a Golden Age of democratic consolidation. But it was also a time when the staggering pace of change fueled new concerns about the genuine health of many newly democratic governments.

Today, confidence in the forward march of democracy is dimming. Scholars speak grimly of how democracies are suffering from "undertow," "rollback," "recession," and even "depression." Others worry that democracies are hollowing themselves out and becoming "partial," "low-intensity," "empty," and "illiberal." In these cases, elections still take place, but civil liberties and checks on power are flouted.

Moreover, the failure of the 2003-2005 "color revolutions" in Georgia, Ukraine, and Kyrgyzstan were highly demoralizing, as was the failure of the 2010-2011 Arab Spring in Egypt, Libya, Syria, and elsewhere in the Middle East and North Africa. Even more recently, authoritarian governance in new democracies such as Hungary, Poland, and Turkey, and in old democracies such as the US, have set off alarm bells. And an unrelenting flood of negative headlines in other democracies has reinforced the sense that illiberalism and nationalist populism are resurgent. Watchdog groups such as Freedom House are convinced that the world has become increasingly less free.

A spate of new books has added to the creeping sense of doom. In *How Democracies Die*, Steven Levitsky and Daniel Ziblatt of Harvard University argue that democracies usually end not with a bang, but with a whimper, as demagogues like President Donald Trump in the US gradually undermine checks and balances.

Likewise, in *The People vs. Democracy*, Harvard's Yascha Mounk warns that liberal democracy is giving way to "undemocratic liberalism" and "illiberal democracy." The former protects basic rights but delegates real power to unelected technocratic bodies like the European Commission. The latter features democratically elected leaders who ignore minority rights. More generally, Mounk and others fear that young people, including in the West, are turning away from democracy.

What the Data Shows

And yet there is reason to doubt that democracy is in retreat around the world. For starters, there is no clear evidence of a dramatic decline in support for democracy across most countries, including in the US. This does not mean that today's uptick in the number of autocracies should be ignored; but it does suggest that the elegies for democracy may be premature.

Polls that show declining global support for democracy should also be interpreted with some skepticism. After all, it is hard to discern people's appetite for democracy in countries ruled by authoritarian regimes, where respondents must be careful about publicly declaring such positions.

In fact, research from the Center for Systemic Peace's Polity Project suggests that the great third wave of democratization, far from receding, may eventually give way to a fourth wave. As of 2015, the latest year for which Polity Project data are available, there were 103 democracies worldwide, accounting for over half of the global population.

Add the 17 countries classified as more democratic than autocratic, and the share of the population living in democracies increases to two-thirds. By comparison, a mere 1% of the population lived in democratic countries in the early 1800s. Even when acknowledging that there are many shades of democratic governance, this statistic alone should give pause to democracy's doomsayers.

To be sure, the resilience of democracy must not become a source of complacency. The continued spread of democratic governance is far from guaranteed. When disaggregated by levels of pluralism, political participation, and respect for civil liberties, several democracies show unmistakable signs of backsliding. According to the Economist Intelligence Unit's *Democracy Index*, just 19 countries, most of them in Western Europe, can be described as "full democracies," as opposed to "flawed democracies," "hybrid regimes," or "authoritarian regimes." Of the 167 countries in the index, 89 registered signs of deterioration in 2017 compared to the previous year.

Among the countries slipping toward authoritarianism are a few recent democratic converts such as the so-called Visegrád Group: the Czech Republic, Hungary, Poland, and Slovakia. The Philippines, led by another illiberal populist, Rodrigo Duterte, is steadily removing liberal constraints. Some of the populist leaders in these countries have taken inspiration from other elected strongmen, such as Recep Tayyip Erdoğan in Turkey and Vladimir Putin in Russia.

These countries' experiences show that, while democracy is still favored by most of the world, it is hardly the only model of government. Likewise, theocracies in the Islamic world and authoritarian capitalism in China offer alternatives that are attractive to autocrats and populists because they can generate certain economic advantages in the short term.

Democracy's Lasting Promise

Still, in the face of all these existential threats, it is worth remembering that democracy has been so successful not just because of procedural institutions such as elections or checks and balances, despite how crucial these institutions are. It could be, to paraphrase Winston Churchill, that despite its many flaws, democracy is still preferable to the alternatives. Democracies, after all, allow people to dismiss their representatives without resorting to bloodshed.

As John Mueller of Ohio State University notes, well-governed liberal democracies give people the freedom "to complain, to petition, to organize, to protest, to demonstrate, to strike, to threaten to emigrate or secede, to shout, to publish, to export their funds, to express a lack of confidence." And, even better, the "government will tend to respond to the sounds of the shouters." Mueller reminds us that even the most mature liberal democracies are works in progress that need constant grooming and improvement. At the most basic level, successful democracies are those that protect the citizenry from violence and the seductive airs of strongmen claiming that they alone represent the people.

For a democracy (be it presidential, parliamentary, or constitutional-monarchical) to flourish, citizens must be convinced that it is a better alternative to theocracy, the divine right of kings, colonial paternalism, or authoritarian rule. Over the past few centuries, people around the world came to recognize that it is, and the idea of liberal democracy thus became contagious.

Despite their limitations, democracies have proved remarkably effective at curbing the more sinister instincts of governments. Consider human rights, which have been widely codified since 1948, when the United Nations adopted the *Universal Declaration of Human Rights*. One might similarly reflect on capital punishment, which used to be the global norm. The latest projections suggest that capital punishment could be abolished completely around the world in less than a decade.

Such profound changes are a reminder of why we must fight for free and fair elections, the rights of minorities, freedom of the press, and the rule of law. While many democracies have faced a crisis of confidence in recent years, their extraordinary victories—and their continuing superiority to the alternatives—continue to represent grounds for optimism.

The Surge of Populism Spells the End of Neoliberalism, Not Liberal Democracy

Sandra Waddock

Sandra Waddock is the Galligan Chair of Strategy and the Carroll School Scholar of Corporate Responsibility at Boston College.

Neoliberalism, the dominant narrative guiding Western democracies and their economies for almost 70 years, is crumbling all around us.

It was set up to protect our freedoms. But neoliberalism's excesses and failures—from recent financial crises to soaring levels of income inequality—have fueled populist movements that threaten not only open markets and free trade but the very freedoms it was meant to safeguard.

The U.K.'s vote for Brexit, the U.S. election of Donald Trump and the rise of both right- and left-wing populism across Europe all point to a desire for change from the established order and a more equitable distribution of the world's wealth. But in each case the popularly chosen remedy is worse than the disease it's intended to cure.

Neoliberalism emerged from the ashes of World World II when a group of economists, politicians, philosophers and others gathered at a ski resort in Switzerland convinced that more open markets would help protect the freedoms threatened by fascism.

With those ideas now discredited, and fascism once again on the rise, it's past time to devise a new narrative to guide our economies in a way that prevents neoliberalism's excesses, promotes universal well-being as an economic imperative and ensures nationalism doesn't once again win the battle of ideas.

While a narrative may not seem like much, my research suggests how important such narratives and their underlying "memes" are in fostering the kind of system change we need right now.

The Old Narrative

Ask any business or economics student what the purpose of a company is. Most likely you will get the same answer: to maximize shareholder wealth.

This narrow view is deeply embedded in the thinking of business school professors and economists and, as a result, of the manager-wannabes they teach.

Yet it is highly problematic, since there are many other groups besides investors whose contributions to the business are as necessary and valuable. Think employees, customers, communities and suppliers, to name a few. Even General Electric's former CEO Jack Welch, the one-time "father" of shareholder wealth maximization, claimed in 2009 that it was "the dumbest idea in the world."

Yet shareholder wealth maximization still dominates economic thinking, and it is a direct result of those neoliberal ideas that emerged from that Swiss mountainside.

How the Old Narrative Was Made

The perspective that companies exist to maximize shareholder wealth is most often attributed to now-deceased economist Milton Friedman. Friedman's arguments, embedded in virtually all economics textbooks, derive from the work of a relatively little-known group of economists, philosophers and historians.

This group, including Friedman, met at Mont Pelerin, Switzerland in 1947 to grapple with the expansion of government interventions they claimed threatened freedom, dignity and particularly free enterprise. They developed the narrative we know as neoliberalism or neoclassical economics. This narrative now dominates global understanding of what economies and businesses do and why they exist, not to mention the nightly news (via constant markets coverage).

The Mont Pelerin Society, whose members included economist Friedrich von Hayek, philosopher Karl Popper and economist George Stigler, agreed on a few core ideas and then crafted them into a resonant story about the purpose of business and how economies—and, ultimately, the world—ought to work.

They acted individually in their own countries to foster freedom and private rights, uphold the functioning of markets and create a globalized order that safeguarded peace and liberty. Some went on to hold positions of power and others had great influence over those who wielded it, such as President Ronald Reagan and U.K. Prime Minister Margaret Thatcher, who embraced Friedman's ideas and ushered in the "maximize shareholder wealth" era for companies.

The result of the Mont Pelerin Society's work is a set of familiar memes, or core units of culture.

Memes and Markets

Unlike internet memes, which spread via the worldwide web, the memes I'm talking about refer to ideas, phrases, symbols and images that replicate from person to person when they resonate, and are ubiquitous. Our common understandings, belief systems and the stories that we tell ourselves about how the world works are based on such memes.

Memes are, I recently argued, an overlooked and vitally important aspect of system change. Recognizable memes form the basis of today's dominant economic narrative: free markets, free trade and globalization, private property, competition, individual but not shared responsibility, and maximization of company and shareholder wealth.

The success of these memes speaks to why business students so readily identify the purpose of the business as maximizing shareholder wealth and with the language of free markets and trade. They are simple, identifiable and based on laudable values like freedom and individual responsibility, after all: things that

Americans in particular, with their individualistic orientation, can readily identify with.

Their power to convey the underlying economic "story" illustrates why change that seems to astute observers to be necessary —change toward more sustainability, dealing with climate change and fostering greater equity—is so difficult. Neoliberalism's pursuit of endless growth, efficiency and free trade have led to setbacks in curbing climate change, enhancing sustainability and reducing inequality, all of which are potentially existential crises for humanity.

In other words, those changes don't fit neatly into market logic because they include both social and ecological values in addition to economic ones. Thus, neoliberalism can't absorb them. Successful memes resonate broadly and are difficult to change unless other, equally successful ones replace them.

Such complex and "wicked problems" are difficult to resolve because there are just too many groups and individuals with different ideas about what the problem is and what caused it, and how to best deal with it.

How to Bring About System Change

Recent work with colleagues on how to bring about large system change to cope with such problems suggests that there is really no way to plan or control such change.

What is needed, as happened with the creation of neoliberalism's core narrative, is that a new set of memes framing a new economic and societal narrative needs to be established. An emerging group called Leading for Wellbeing and composed of global organizations, universities and newspapers is attempting to do just this, built on the notion that the world's major institutions and businesses should "operate in service of well-being and dignity for all."

Tomorrow's narrative needs to be framed very differently from today's. It needs to recognize that economies are part of societies and nature but not the only important thing. A new narrative should frame the purpose of business very differently, taking different stakeholders and the natural environment into account. It could also provide a more reasonable and effective basis for resolving the key crises of our time, such as the warming planet and the growing gap between rich and poor.

Companies could, as business professors Tom Donaldson and Jim Walsh recently argued, focus on producing collective value, rather than simply shareholder wealth.

Dignity and well-being can be enhanced, for instance, by emphasizing job creation and stability, fair wages and fair markets, rather than financial wealth, efficiency and growth. Measures like the Genuine Progress Indicator would incorporate well-being and individual dignity into the measure of an economy, as opposed to merely its activity, making it a great substitute for GDP or GNP.

If we hope to overcome this tide of populism and nationalism sweeping the West, a new, more powerful narrative is desperately needed—a new story that proves more compelling than the one that brought Trump and populists in Europe to power.

Organizations to Contact

The editors have compiled the following list of organizations concerned with the issues debated in this book. The descriptions are derived from materials provided by the organizations. All have publications or information available for interested readers. This list was compiled on the date of publication of the present volume; the information provided here may change. Be aware that many organizations take several weeks or longer to respond to inquiries, so allow as much time as possible.

American Enterprise Institute (AEI)
1789 Massachusetts Avenue NW
Washington, DC 20036
phone: (202) 862-5800
website: www.aei.org

Founded in 1943, the American Enterprise Institute (AEI) is a research and advocacy organization dedicated to promoting democracy, free enterprise, and American global leadership. AEI scholars conduct research in a wide variety of fields including economics, education, health care, and foreign policy.

Brookings Institution
1775 Massachusetts Avenue NW
Washington, DC 20036
phone: (202) 797-6000
email: communications@brookings.edu
website: www.brookings.edu

With over three hundred academic and government experts, the Brookings Institution is one of the premier policy think tanks in the United States. Brookings experts conduct research on foreign policy, economics, development, and governance and provide policy recommendations based on that research.

Center for Migration Studies (CMS)
307 East 60th Street, 4th Floor
New York, NY 10022
phone: (212) 337-3080
email: cms@cmsny.org
website; www.cmsny.org/

The Center for Migration Studies (CMS) is a think tank and an educational institute devoted to the study of human migration. CMS works to promote understanding between immigrants and receiving communities, and to public policies that safeguard the dignity and rights of migrants and refugees. CMS is a member of the Scalabrini International Migration Network (SIMN), a global network of migrant shelters and service centers, and the Scalabrini Migration Study Centers, a network of think tanks on international migration and refugee protection.

Center for the Study of Nationalism – University of Oklahoma (CSN)
David L. Boren College of International Studies
Farzaneh Hall, Room 107
729 Elm Ave.
Norman, OK 73019
phone: (405) 325-1396
email: cis@ou.edu
website: www.ou.edu/cis/sponsored_programs/center-for-the-study-of-nationalism

The Center for the Study of Nationalism (CSN) connects faculty and students at the University of Oklahoma to the empirical and theoretical aspects of studying nationalism and related issues including cultural authenticity, ethnic conflict and civil war, immigration and citizenship, globalization, development, and inequality.

European Centre for International Political Economy (ECIPE)
Avenue des Arts 40,
1040 Brussels
Belgium
phone: +32 (0)2 289 1350
email: info@ecipe.org
website: www.ecipe.org

The European Centre for International Political Economy (ECIPE) is an independent, nonprofit think tank dedicated to the study of European economic issues. ECIPE advocates for free trade and the progressive reduction of economic barriers as a path toward greater peace, prosperity, and security across the globe.

Migration Policy Institute (MPI)
1400 16th Street NW, Suite 300
Washington, DC 20036
phone: (202) 266-1940
email: info@migrationpolicy.org
website: www.migrationpolicy.org

Founded in 2001, the Migration Policy Institute (MPI) has established itself as a leading institution in the field of migration policy and as a source of authoritative research, learning opportunities, and new policy ideas. MPI maintains a special commitment to work on immigration and integration policies in North America and Europe, where its two offices are located, but it also remains active around the world, taking a global and comparative approach to migration issues when possible.

Peterson Institute for International Economics (PIIE)
1750 Massachusetts Avenue NW
Washington, DC 20036
phone: (202) 328-9000
email: comments@piie.com
website: www.piie.com

The Peterson Institute for International Economics (PIIE) is a private, nonpartisan think tank dedicated to the study of economics, trade policy, and globalization. PIIE conducts research on emerging issues, develops policy ideas, and works to educate government officials, business leaders, and the public on international economic issues.

Pew Research Center
1615 L Street NW, Suite 800
Washington, DC 20003
phone: (202) 419-4300
website: www.pewresearch.org

Pew Research Center is a nonpartisan fact tank that informs the public about the issues, attitudes, and trends shaping the world. It conducts public opinion polling, demographic research, media content analysis, and other empirical social science research. Pew Research Center does not take policy positions.

United States Institute of Peace (USIP)
2301 Constitution Avenue NW
Washington, DC 20037
phone: (202) 457-1700
website: www.usip.org

USIP is America's nonpartisan institute to promote national security and global stability by reducing violent conflicts abroad. Their staff guides peace talks and advises governments; trains police and religious leaders; and supports community groups opposing extremism—all to help troubled countries solve their own conflicts peacefully.

Bibliography

Books

Madeleine Albright. *Fascism: A Warning*. New York, NY: HarperCollins, 2018.

Benedict Anderson. *Imagined Communities: Reflections on the Origin and Spread of Nationalism*. New York, NY: Verso, 1983.

Damon T. Berry. *Blood & Faith: Christianity in American White Nationalism*. Syracuse, NY: Syracuse University Press, 2017.

Ian Bremmer. *Us vs. Them: The Failure of Globalism*. New York, NY: Penguin Random House, 2018.

Patrick Deneen. *Why Liberalism Failed*. New Haven, CT: Yale University Press, 2018.

Roger Eatwell and Matthew Goodwin. *National Populism: The Revolt Against Liberal Democracy*. New York, NY: Penguin Books, 2018.

William A. Galston. *Anti-Pluralism: The Populist Threat to Liberal Democracy*. New Haven, CT: Yale University Press, 2018.

Yoram Hazony. *The Virtue of Nationalism*. New York, NY: Basic Books, 2018.

John B. Judis. *The Nationalist Revival: Trade, Immigration, and the Revolt Against Globalization*. New York, NY: Columbia Global Reports, 2018.

Rich Lowry. *The Case for Nationalism: How It Made Us Powerful, United, and Free*. New York, NY: HarperCollins, 2019.

R. R. Reno. *Return of the Strong Gods: Nationalism, Populism, and the Future of the West.* Washington, DC: Regnery Gates Publishing, 2019.

Vegas Tenold. *Everything You Love Will Burn: Inside the Rebirth of White Nationalism in America.* New York, NY: Nation Books, 2018.

Brad Todd and Salena Zito. *The Great Revolt: Inside the Populist Coalition Reshaping American Politics.* New York, NY: Crown Forum, 2018.

Periodicals and Internet Sources

Colton Carpenter, "Choosing Patriotism over Nationalism," *Harvard Political Review,* April 1, 2019, https://harvardpolitics.com/columns-old/patriotism-over-nationalism/.

Patricia Ehrkamp, "Nativism, Nationalism, and the Hardening Lines of Citizenship," *Society and Space,* July 4, 2017, https://societyandspace.org/2017/07/04/nativism-nationalism-and-the-hardening-lines-of-citizenship/.

Uri Friedman, "What Is a Nativist?" *Atlantic,* April 11, 2017, https://www.theatlantic.com/international/archive/2017/04/what-is-nativist-trump/521355/.

Noam Gidron, "The left shouldn't fear nationalism. It should embrace it." Vox, February 8, 2018, https://www.vox.com/the-big-idea/2018/2/8/16982036/nationalism-patriotism-left-right-trump-democrats-solidarity.

Jared A. Goldstein, "Is There Really a Difference Between Patriotism and Nationalism?" Slate, November 20, 2018, https://slate.com/news-and-politics/2018/11/trump-nationalism-patriotism-difference.html.

Emma Green, "Imagining Post-Trump Nationalism," *Atlantic*, June 30, 2019, https://www.theatlantic.com/politics/archive/2019/06/first-things-nationalism-trump/592996/.

Jozef Andrew Kosc, "The Liberal Roots of Nativism," *Foreign Affairs*, September 29, 2017, https://www.foreignaffairs.com/articles/united-states/2017-09-29/liberal-roots-nativism

Charles Kupchan, "In Europe, Nativism and Nationalism May Be Reaching Their Limits," *Foreign Policy*, September 24, 2019, https://foreignpolicy.com/2019/09/24/in-europe-nativism-and-nationalism-may-be-reaching-their-limits/.

Jill Lepore, "Don't Let Nationalists Speak for the Nation," *New York Times*, May 25, 2019, https://www.nytimes.com/2019/05/25/opinion/sunday/nationalism-liberalism-2020.html

Rick Moran, "Nationalism, Nativism, and Patriotism," PJ Media, October 19, 2017, https://pjmedia.com/trending/nationalism-nativism-patriotism/.

Benjamin E. Park, "The Revolutionary Roots of America's Religious Nationalism," *Religion & Politics*, March 20, 2018, http://religionandpolitics.org/2018/03/20/the-revolutionary-roots-of-americas-religious-nationalism/.

Paul R. Pillar, "The History of American Nationalism," *National Interest*, November 29, 2018, https://nationalinterest.org/blog/paul-pillar/history-american-nationalism-37597.

Sudhanva D. Shetty, "There's A World of Difference Between Patriotism And Nationalism," Huffington Post, July 3, 2016, https://www.huffingtonpost.in/sudhanva-d-shetty/patriotism-nationalism-a-_b_9354822.html.

Linton Weeks, "America's Love Affair with Nationalism," NPR, September 28, 2011, https://www.npr.org/2011/09/28/140869378/americas-love-affair-with-nationalism.

Index